COMPUTER SCIENCE, TECHNOLOGY, AND APPLICATIONS

PRACTICE AND RESEARCH NOTES IN RELATIONAL DATABASE APPLICATIONS

COMPUTER SCIENCE, TECHNOLOGY, AND APPLICATIONS

Additional books in this series can be found on Nova's website under the Series tab.

Additional E-books in this series can be found on Nova's website under the E-books tab.

COMPUTER SCIENCE, TECHNOLOGY, AND APPLICATIONS

PRACTICE AND RESEARCH NOTES IN RELATIONAL DATABASE APPLICATIONS

HAITAO YANG

Novinka
Nova Science Publishers, Inc.
New York

NOTICE TO THE READER

The Publisher has taken reasonable care in the preparation of this book, but makes no expressed or implied warranty of any kind and assumes no responsibility for any errors or omissions. No liability is assumed for incidental or consequential damages in connection with or arising out of information contained in this book. The Publisher shall not be liable for any special, consequential, or exemplary damages resulting, in whole or in part, from the readers' use of, or reliance upon, this material.

Independent verification should be sought for any data, advice or recommendations contained in this book. In addition, no responsibility is assumed by the publisher for any injury and/or damage to persons or property arising from any methods, products, instructions, ideas or otherwise contained in this publication.

This publication is designed to provide accurate and authoritative information with regard to the subject matter covered herein. It is sold with the clear understanding that the Publisher is not engaged in rendering legal or any other professional services. If legal or any other expert assistance is required, the services of a competent person should be sought. FROM A DECLARATION OF PARTICIPANTS JOINTLY ADOPTED BY A COMMITTEE OF THE AMERICAN BAR ASSOCIATION AND A COMMITTEE OF PUBLISHERS.

LIBRARY OF CONGRESS CATALOGING-IN-PUBLICATION DATA

Available upon Request
ISBN: 978-1-61668-850-9

Published by Nova Science Publishers, Inc. ✛ *New York*

CONTENTS

PREFACE

Relational database applications cover such a great variety of subjects and cases that professionals from the software industries or researchers on the fields of database studies might encounter at the same time distinct issues based on DBMS. *Practice and Research Notes in Relational Database Applications* consists of two parts—

Its first part concerns the data synchronization issue of heterogeneous DBMSs across distributed devices and autonomic systems on Internet. The book present a detailed description of designing a generic sync middleware system, GSMS, and provides in-depth coverage of key topics including that, sync network, schemes for capturing and logging data change, change propagation, sync session optimization, etc. A series of GSMS tests are exemplified for several mainstream DBMS products, e.g., Oracle 9i, Sybase ASE 12.5, MS SQL server 7.0.

The second part is contributed to the study of Relational Schema Representation for Complex Charts, RSRCC. This issue arises from many desktop or office applications where complex heading charts are often assumed for intuitive and explanatory descriptions of facts, rules, or items in multiple dimensions, when these charts are required to be used in a MIS application that builds on a RDBMS, they need to be represented equitably in form of relational schema. The process of mapping charts into relation tables can be regarded largely as a reverse process of mapping multidimensional data model into data cubes or two-dimension tables via SQL statistical calculation, though the later process has been studied intensively in the field of multidimensional database for quite a long time, the former topic still lacks comprehensive investigation. To fill in this gap, the book presents a systematic approach to RSRCC directly for or heuristically for most common cases.

PART I. GSMS—A HETEROGENEOUS DATA SYNC SOLUTION

ABSTRACT

The development of information technology is closely related to the requirements from social and economic progress, after the 21st century, mainstream professionals and organizations are rapidly moving into a new era of information society, which are featured with enabling feasible access to data services at any time, any site via devices at hand, this is the ideal of ubiquitous computing which is advocated first by IT pioneers and academic community, later becomes widely prevalent in IT industries and the mainstream public society. An important basis of ubiquitous computing application lies on the guarantee of reliable and fast access to data resources, of which a common and fundamental measure is distributed deployment of data replicas. Besides, in the one hand, more and more cooperative applications among different organizations are emerging today, while participating companies are often reluctant to give up the autonomy of data management of own side; in fact, most of cooperators prefer that their data applications are based on local replicas which are safer and fast accessible. As a result, there arises the data sync issue cross different replicas. Data sync can be also viewed in the light of the so-called Forwards Eventually-Consistent Transaction, in short FECT, in which the intermediate inconsistent status must be tolerated for a relatively long interval, otherwise, the chance of the process being complete is very low. Data sync (DS) is a typical FECT, in which data changes are propagated across all replicas in order to refresh replicas into a consistent version forwards, while a roll-back approach is not applicable since the source replica of committed data change reflecting a new status of the modeled reality, should not and usually can not be set back to its previous status. DS solutions can be approached on three tiers: 1) application's, 2) database system's, and 3) middleware's, among them the first approach is tightly coupled with specific applications, thus is inflexible, the second one is less flexible but tightly relies on database products from the same vendor as the solution provider, only the third one is both flexible and suitable for DS across heterogeneous database systems. Normally conform to standard protocols is a preferential selection in the practice of generic software design and so is for DS, thus, a work of DS middleware, which accords with the OMA SyncML protocols – a series of DS protocols for pervasive computing, is presented as the main content in this chapter to illustrate FECT applications.

Chapter 1

INTRODUCTION

The so-called data synchronization, in short DS or *data sync*, is referred to as a propagation process of data renewal across distributed replicas. The terms *data sync* and *data replication* are often mistaken for each other. However, a *replication* without any modifier implies a unilateral propagation somehow, and cares less about the timeliness and schedule literally, but a *sync* tends to mean a bilateral peer process and express a meaning of timeliness literally. Nevertheless, they are often interchangeable in situations that their differences lead to no confusion. In the matter of transaction processing, data replication has two basic approaches: one is via synchronous mode, and the other is via asynchronous mode. The propagation process is regarded as one transaction as a whole by the former approach, but separated into a series of small transactions by the latter. Synchronous mode often has a pretty low ratio of success, this is a big problem, and thus it is seldom adopted in practice [1]. When the progress of data renewal are more important than the strict consistency of transaction, or partial renewals are better than none, the forwards eventual consistency should substitute the atomicity of all-or-nothing and become the practical demand of transactions of data sync [2], it is this situation that makes distributed DS become a typical FECT. In this chapter, research on such a FECT is presented with the development of Generic Sync Middleware System for heterogeneous DBMS on Internet – in short, GSMS.

Demands for GSMS-alike products mainly come from the diversities of DBMS distributed applications and the increase of information exchange and share. With the rapid development of pervasive computing, industrial and academic societies are seeking better fundamental solutions for DS across distributed devices and autonomic systems. However, most of the existing solutions are far from the classical technical ideal [3] that is featured by the well-known Date's 12 Rules [4], particularly the sixth rule: data replication transparency – summarized by C.J. Date, a famous pioneer of relational database, in 1987. In accord with these rules is a real challenge in developing GSMS-alike products for a variety of requirements cross from traditional applications to the pervasive computing that refers to numerous diverse heterogeneous client-ends. Indeed, the development of GSMS should refer to research achievements for traditional data replication applications [2, 5] as well as utilize the free software resources in mobile data sync applications [6].

Before going to the development of GSMS, we should review related research for reference in advance. Firstly, on the aspect of DS consistency, J. Gray et al [1] told us that synchronous mode is not realistic due to its poor success ratios. While R.Gallersdörfer and M.Nicola [2] suggested relaxing the requirement of consistency to gain better performance, and H.Yu and A.Vahdat [7] considered that for most Internet scenarios the service availability is worthy of sacrificing strict consistency between data replicas. Secondly, on the aspect of renewal propagation, the research results of literature [8] and [9] foreshowed that a tree topology has the advantage of low costs. Thirdly, with respect to the middleware, traditional frameworks of middleware implementation which are indicated by work of Armendáriz-Iñigo et al [10] often impose a bottleneck on the response performance of DMBS which hosts the middleware: because the middleware is inserted as an intermediate layer into between the client applications and the supporting DBMS, thus it intercepts all access requests for the DBMS [11]. Customers and DBMS vendors are not willing to see such a scenario occurs, not only due to the bottleneck problem bus also middleware's coupling-tightly with the concrete expansion mechanism of DBMS products.

Then, as for the industrial products of data sync: being driven by the strong demands from the market, major communication vendors (over 650 companies) have jointly raised a platform-independent data sync standard, SyncML[1], as the generic framework for information exchange across any networks and any devices [12]. SyncML-based standard and generic middleware products of data sync are, however, still falling short of requirements for a generic solution of DS applications built on mainstream RDBMS (relational DBMS) [13]. Even more, small and medium enterprises

---

[1] SyncML is now referred to as OMA DS & DM (Open Mobile Alliance Data Synchronization and Device Management), by convention and for succinctness, we prefer the old name for it.

require DS products being low-priced, easily deployed, capable of free-configuration, and independent of any specific DBMS vendors.

Finally, let us review the open sources side of SyncML-based DS middleware, of which the sync4j project [6] is perhaps the most well known, but the applicability of sync4j is not so convincing since: 1) it alters all data tables participating DS; 2) it does not universally handle the diversity and abundance of data types of various RDBMS products; 3) it lacks the capacity of heterogeneous type mapping. In fact, sync4j has not offered DS function across heterogeneous RDBMSs yet.

Big problems of DS solutions come from the generality and nonintervention first, and then the performance and conflict reconciliation; thus, solutions on the system architecture and design model level are most wanted instead of practical engineering techniques in this field.

Chapter 2

TECHNICAL FOCUS

As to the product level implementation of GSMS-alike middleware, the consideration of the system architecture and sync mode comes first, which should avoid the above mentioned deficiency of classical middleware and the intervention to data applications as in sync4j, and then the disposal of common tasks of DS software follows. The routine problems in DS include the granularity selection of data object managed, tracking and recording data changes, sync information maintenance crossing sync nodes, ensuring no-missing propagations of data changes, disposing of otherness from heterogeneous DBMSs, etc. Normally, the common tasks of DS are classified into two big categories: 1) change capture, and 2) remote update. From the point of performance and practicability, the efficiency of change-capture mechanism and the suitability of change-propagation disposal are essential for GSMS. The change-capture mechanism counts for much to the design of middleware, while the change-propagation disposal rests with the layout of sync protocol implementation and sync topology. Besides, the optimization of change-propagation is also important, e.g. when an *operation transfer* mode is adopted [5], the differences between dialects of DML (Data Manipulation Language) should be well dealt with much cares, and the idempotency and repetitions of manipulation should be taken into account, while a *content transfer* mode is assumed [5], sync record sets with a large amount of data should undertake a logical partition [14], and a meta-description and semantic explanation of data changes must be provisioned. In addition, other issues such as the overheads of sync system running and maintenance, concurrent control and exception handling, etc. should be in the list of concerns, too.

Chapter 3

ROUTE OF DEVELOPING GSMS

First of all, certain design principles are ruled: 1) using sync topologies under which sync network configuration is simple and flexible, malfunction detection is easy, sync correlation is succinct, network transmission load is light, and access paths are convenient to manage; 2) less intervention in higher level client applications; 3) extendable to new RDBMSs; and 4) applicable to client ends of limited resources. Then, we define the applicable scope of GSMS – for RDBMSs that support standard SQL and provision trigger mechanism for basic data manipulations.

According to the above principles, the desirable GSMS is a loosely combined system that adopts SyncML as the propagation protocol for data change and appears as an add-on middleware. The add-on middleware is distinguished from the traditional one [11] in the way: it does not act as the entrance or agent of the hosting RDBMS any more, is purely an add-on software which works in parallel with the hosting RDBMS. The key to such an architecture implementation is by separating GSMS into two parts: 1) one is inside the hosting RDBMS, which is composed of triggers and store procedures, its main function is change-capture; and 2) the other is outside the hosting RDBMS, which consists of software components programmed by procedure languages, it is responsible for the change propagation & reception tasks. Although trigger mechanism is an extension to standard SQL functions, today it has been provided as a built-in basic function by all major RDBMS products, and is widely supported by more and more others, with which data application software can gain a system level support from DBMS to work with routine procedures of DBMS in parallel. Of course, a trigger has some programming limits, such as it cannot directly call for programs outside the hosting DBMS, no program parameters are allowed, etc. Besides, the execution efficiency of triggers is also a focused problem. As to the compatibility and openness, usually a JDBC access mode is recommended for the outer components of GSMS. As a result, whenever GSMS needs to be applied to a new RDBMS, only the inner part of GSMS needs development, that is, several program templates of trigger and store procedure of the new RDBMS are required for change-capture. Of course, for easy deployment of cross OS platform, JAVA program language is the best option for developing both DS client and server since its sync client and server can be placed in different OS platform via JVM (Java Virtual Machine). Sync clients should be light-weighted, while sync servers must provide much stronger function to fulfill rather complex tasks, such as conflict reconciliation.

Chapter 4

GSMS ARCHITECTURE

Since the 1960s, software engineering technology has experienced from simple structured programming to software pattern exploiture and component based development, consequently software reuse becomes one of the most wanted merits. The software component concept refers to a fuzzy object in general since its boundary definition varies according to the desirable granulation and scope of component management for concrete applications; however, indeed there is roughly a common agreement for component classification: 1) by modality; 2) by usage; and 3) by function layering – fundamental, intermediate, and domain-specific layers; etc. Most often people prefer the function classification of software components. Components from fundamental layer are used for provision of basic and supporting functions that are associated directly with OS and DBMS, while domain-specific layer's components provide application-oriented functions. Whereas components from the intermediate layer, i.e. intermediate components, are for facility and agent services, normally of which the coupling with OS and DBMS is looser than that of components from the fundamental layer, and is not confined to specific application – GSMS should be positioned on this layer. Intermediate components can be regarded as middleware [15] in a narrow sense, though, more precisely, middleware refers to software that is common to multiple applications and builds on the network transport services to enable ready development of new applications and network services – by Xian-He Sun, Illinois Institute of Technology, and Argonne National Laboratory (http://www.cs.iit.edu/~sun/).

Traditional middleware is designed for working in a broker pattern, and usually is deployed between client-oriented applications and support software.

Most of existing DS middleware acts as a pre-positive processor in front of synced DBMS: intercepts client requests for database, and forwards them to the target DBMS instance after necessary analysis and preprocess. This serial process pattern might not only decrease the throughput of DBMS products, but also potentially overlap with industrial ODBC standards, and could become incompatible with future evolvement of ODBC products. Therefore, as mention in Section 3 an add-on pattern is suggested for GSMS middleware here, the structure is showed in Figure 1. More details about such a GSMS design are discussed in the next section.

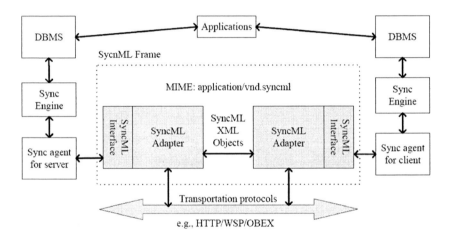

Figure 1. An architecture of add-on middleware for GSMS.

Chapter 5

SYNC MODEL

There are four basic tasks on sync disposal of distributed data: deployment management of sync nodes, data change capture, data change propagation, and conflict detection and handling. These aspects should be considered in details on any concrete implementation of GSMS. At first, as a kind of distributed system GSMS should have its connection topology well-planned [7] to decrease the repetition or overlapping of data change propagation, lower the requirement for computing capacity of intermediate nodes, and minimize the cost of propagation, etc. Especially, sync topology is appropriate or may not have a direct influence on users experience in pervasive computing across wireless base stations serving for a great number of mobile customers [8, 9]. Next, it is required of high adaptability to heterogeneous DBMSs, not relying on specific vendors' DBMS products, but assuming a widely-supported industrial standard – best on the level of data schema or API, thus, the SyncML data sync protocol is selected [16, 17, 18]. Thirdly, the capture of data change should be automated, and its implementation should not alter existing designs of higher-level data applications, and can avoid occupying busy resources that are accessed frequently by system processes of DBMS. Fourthly, the data propagation should be reliable, particularly, avoid cascaded aborts, and the effect of each finished transfer between a pair of nodes should be durable. Finally, it can apply to mobile ends with limited computing capacity.

Among the above-mentioned four tasks, the conflict reconciliation is the hardest for automatic handling, since it often required of rather complete semantics about data change. Therefore, it had better lower the possibility of conflict occurrence, of which useful analyses are often appropriate for specific scenarios only.

As soon as an event of data change is recorded in local persistent memories, the event's effect should be eventually propagated to all other nodes to be synced if the durability of propagation process is guaranteed. If an event of data change is missed, however, then its result might get lost forever at worst, unless another sync event that covers the same data object is ignited afterwards. Thereby, the task of data change capture should be fulfilled in a higher reliability. From the point of view of software engineering, achieving such a target certainly needs a tradeoff. Compared with the implementation of data change propagation, of which the design pattern is basically defined if SyncML protocol is adopted, the fulfillment of data change capture is more challenging. Up to now, basic approaches for change capture can be summed up as follows,

- *Snapshot method (assumed by Oracle [19], SQL Server [20])*
- *Trigger method (Oracle Symmetric Replication) [19]*
- *Logging method (Sybase [21], DB2[22], SQL Server [20])*
- *API method (SynchroLogic's SyncKit [23])*
- *Shadow method (DataSync [24])*
- *Control table change method (PDRE [25])*

After referring to the merits and defects of these methods, we recommend that syncretizing the trigger mechanism and control table change method, because the former has an advantage of no change missing, and the later has an advantage of no intervening in applications. Now our basic sync model can be outlined.

According to fundamental tasks, a GSMS can be divided into four subsystems:

1. sync configuration
2. change capture
3. propagation
4. conflict handling
5. replica renewal

Sometimes, subsystems 3 plus 5 are regarded as sync system in a narrow sense. Today, component-building methods are often assumed by most of IDEs (integrated development environments), thus, module capsulations are a necessary stage of coding processes. For example, all operations related closely to DBMS are capsulated in a module named *SyncSource*, which carries out basic DML operations such *iNsert*, *Delete*, *Update*, etc., and is apt to be extended later. The module illustration of GSMS admin facility is showed in Figure 2.

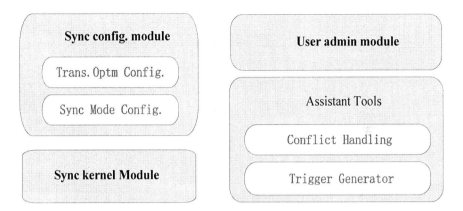

Figure 2. Basic modules of GSMS admin tools.

The concept model of GSMS basic units are given as follows,

- *Data-node: a device where data objects reside, which is capable of hosting data.*
- *Sync-client: the role in implementing SyncML protocol, which issues request messages [16].*
- *Sync-server: the role in implementing SyncML protocol, which handles request messages and responds with response messages [16].*
- *Both the sync-client and sync-server are called the **sync ends**.*
- *Sync-node: a **device** where **sync ends** are deployed.*

In DS applications, data-node must be assigned to and synced through concrete sync-node. Normally, a sync-node is geographically close to the data-nodes it serves, e.g. they are all located in a same LAN. Commonly, a data-node and its assigned sync-node are considered as a whole, thus they are together referred to as a *node*.

Replica: a homogeneous instance of the data object referred. There are temporary discrepancies among different replicas, but eventually they should become identical in content. In relational data model, different replicas of the same data object should coincide with each other in the set of concerned attributes, despite that this attribute set might be contained in different relational schemas distributed over different nodes. In cases without confusion, nodes can be used to refer to replicas.

A basic *sync activity* indicates a direct sync interaction between a pair of nodes or replicas. According to SyncML protocol, as to each basic sync activity one of the pair of synced nodes should be stipulated as the server end or node.

Sync-wave refers to a series of subsequent sync activities, which reflects a whole course of specific version of data; intuitively, it looks like a propagation of water wave. When two sync-waves meet, they will merge into a sync-wave of new round, and the new sync-wave carries the data contents that are out of conflict (originally consistent or agreed on), whereas data contents in conflict are left behind. The path a sync-wave passes is called a *trace* of sync-wave.

Trigger mechanism provides a standard built-in procedure entrance of DBMS, which ignites the user-defined SQL scripts to run inside the DBMS whenever any associated data manipulation event occurs on DML level.

Hierarchy-Star (HS) topology refers to a DS topology structure of connected stars topologies, where stars are joined through their hub nodes that play two roles: one is as the server in the original star topology, and the other is as a client in the HS.

HS topology is often adopted in mobile applications and pervasive computing regarding that, 1) the asymmetry of diverse devices' capacities, 2) as to the end users the available communication resources are de facto restrained to the assigned channel to the current hub, which cannot go beyond the specific hierarchy, and 3) loop paths are prohibited in Internet. Thus, in our sync model, nodes can sync actively with only one node on the higher hierarchy–such a node is called the intermediate node, and then tree topology is formed. The tree topology has the merit of low transit cost and easy management [9]. To emphasize the hierarchy of nodes, see Figure 3, we prefer to call the above formed tree topology as *hierarchy-star* topology, in short HS topology. Under the module programming principle, in the intermediate node that functions as both server and client, we deploy both a sync-server component and a client-client component instead of a compound component combining the server and client functions. In this case, the sync-client behaves like a usual data application in the intermediate node. This intermediate node deployment has the merits of configuration flexibility and module independency.

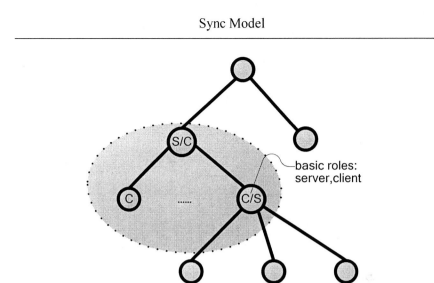

Figure 3. Hierarchy-star topology.

Propagation unit of data change refers to the minimum logical container of data change to be transferred, which should be no larger than a data record and no smaller than the primary key.

Content transfer: it is the content of data change that will be propagated for data version propagations [5], which is preferred for data change caused by *Insert* or *Update* manipulations.

Operation transfer: it is the DML statements with the necessary data object identity (e.g. the primary key and its values) that will be propagated for data version propagations, which is preferred for data change caused by *Delete* manipulations.

Change-log refers to the specific table in RDBMS for storing the data change information captured. The record of data change will be deleted from the source change-log whenever it arrives at the target node, which is safe in a HS sync topology though but may not sure in others. The change-log scheme has the advantage of no interference in higher-level applications, but at the cost of store redundancy of data information. This scheme is first assumed by PeerDirect [25] for the PDRE system. In contrast, *sync4j* records the data change information in an additional field of the data table, which is equivalent to merging the corresponding fields of the change-log table into all data tables that take part in the DS, thus it would necessitate re-programming legacy applications otherwise *Insert* manipulations could not be executed as before due to those later added fields, and cannot record directly any *Delete* manipulations since the hosted record is gone (deleted). Hereafter, records from a change-log table are called *change records*.

Snapshot: if the local consistency of replicas in a node is guaranteed, then the global instant status (intermediate) of all sync replicas can be regarded as a snapshot of all sync-waves and nodes' status at that very time point.

Refining unit of change-capture: in RDBMS, the minimal unit of data change is field. Most of prevailing DBMSs, e.g. MySQL 5.0, Oracle9i, offer in their triggers *New* or *Old* alike delimiters to indicate that the prefixed field's value is before or after the manipulation. Through comparing the New and Old values, we can detect if the value of a field of common data type has been changed by an *Update* manipulation, thus to refine the data object's granulation down to the field level. Such refining can lower the possibility of sync conflict, and decrease the amount of transferring data at a bit delay in the response of Update manipulations. As for sensing a change of fields of special type, such as Oracle's blob fields, usually DBMS products require that applications should update a common type field as well. Our GSMS provides a GUI for selecting configurations of change-capture units on field/table levels.

Configuring sync objects: DBA (database administer) at each node should tell GSMS which database and which data tables will take part in or quit DS. In this stage, the information about table structure, including the primary key, the names and data types of the fields to be synced, should be registered in GSMS, and the mapping relations between each pair of sync tables are also required established.

Frequency of sync: in general, the fast data changes are propagated, the lower the probabilities of inconsistencies among different replicas will be, but the higher the frequency of sync and the expenditure of running sync systems, especially when most of related data applications are write-intensive [5].

Baseline of sync: the actually necessitated sync content, which refers to, in the *incremental mode*, the data units that have been known changed after last successful sync, whereas in the *total mode*, the whole content from the source replica.

Sync exception: in whatever sync scheme, any field that is non-DML assigned cannot be in the set of sync fields, e.g. the auto-increment column in MS SQL Sever – for such a field the value synced from the change source is invalid. Therefore, we stipulate that such fields be excluded in the sync discussion.

Chapter 6

DESIGN AND MAINTENANCE
OF CHANGE-LOG

Given that, the relation schema of *change-log* is as showed in Table 1, where *SeqN_change* indicates the sequence number of data changes (including modification, deletion, and insertion of data record) within a data table – different data tables should be numbered separately, *change-type* = U | D | N stands for "*Update | Delete | iNsert*" manipulations respectively. In most cases, each basic DML manipulation corresponds to a set of records in the *change-log*, however, the *Update* manipulation that changes any value of the primary key, say *Pkey* cannot be logged directly in the change-log, but since it is equivalent to a *Delete*(Old.*Pkey*) and a *Insert*(New.*Pkey*) manipulation, it can be logged through a set of records corresponding to *Delete*(Old.*Pkey*) and a set of records corresponding to *Insert*(New.*Pkey*) in change-log. Field *chg_lst_fields* stores the list of relation attributes that have been changed since the last sync in an expression of binary string such that each bit stands for an attribute in sequence, and a *Null* value for all attributes. Besides, *SeqN_change* can correlate together the values of the primary key's all attributes for the same data record, which will play a role in refining sync granulation (see Section 7). *Timestamp* indicates the happening time of the current data change; *URI_origin* labels the creator of the current version of a data record, which is different from the *URI_sync* that refers to the neighbor node from which the current data version comes directly, i.e., the direct source of propagation; both *URI_origin* and *Birth_time* together label uniquely the original source of the current change, they are useful for conflict reconciliations of different data versions.

Table 1. The relation schema
of *change-log* [3]

Fields	Description	Node types
Table_name	local name of synced data table	All
SeqN_change	Sequence number of data table's change	All
Key_field	name of a constituent field of primary key	All
StrValue_kf	String expression of Value of *key_field*	All
Change_type	"U	D	N" –*Update, Delete, iNsert* manipulation	All
Chg_lst_fields	fields where data change occurred since last sync	All
Timestamp	Arrival time of the current sync-wave, or occurrence time of local changes	All
URI_sync	Neighbor sync node's URI	Non-leaf
URI _ Origin	Creator's URI of the current sync-wave	Non-leaf
Birth_time	Creating time of the current sync-wave	Non-leaf
Sem	Semaphore for concurrent processing	All

In this section a data table named *table_data* is used as the example to show how an event of data record change is mapped into *change-log*, and how a piece of information for propagation is created from a set of records of *change-log*. Given that, the primary key of *table_data* is $(f_1, f_2, ..., f_k)$, i.e., $\{f_i \mid 1 \le i \le k\}$ is the set of attributes of the primary key, of which the value of any attribute can be expressed in a string of ASII characters (this excludes abnormal data types such as Oracle's lob type), then any value of f_i $\{1 \le i \le k\}$ can be stored in *StrValue_kf*, a field of character-string type, meanwhile the field name, $f_i \{1 \le i \le k\}$ self is stored in the field *Key_field*, that is, each tuple of $(f_i, \text{Str}(f_i))\{1 \le i \le k\}$ is corresponding to a record of *change-log*, here function Str(f) is for translating the value of f into a value of string type. In this design, $\{\text{Str}(f_i) \mid 1 \le i \le k\}$, the primary key's value tuple corresponds to k records under the same value of *SeqN_change*.

When a primary key's value tuple, $\{\text{Str}(f_i) \mid 1 \le i \le k\}$, is used to locate data records in the corresponding data table (remote or local), each $\text{Str}(f_i)\{1 \le i \le k\}$ should be reverted into the value of the data type of f_i $\{1 \le i \le k\}$ in the target DBMS. Normally, sync middlewares should provide a reverting function: for the sender it is a real reversion used to locate a data record undergoing change in the source table, for the receiver it might be just a data type transformation since the local data type might be different from that of the sync source. Triggers need not doing reverting operations; they are just responsible for mapping a data record changed into a set of records in *change-log*.

6.1. PROPAGATION AND MAINTENANCE

Data change needs being packed in form of SyncML messages for transfer. GSMS should put the primary key's value tuple of each changed data record into a child element such as <LocURI> of the <source> element under a command element:

<LocURI><key><f_1>Str(f_1)</f_1><f_2>Str(f_2)</f_2>...<f_k>Str(f_k)</f_k></key></LocURI>

While other data fields should be sent in child elements of the <Data> element. However, when propagating the changes made by *Delete* manipulations, no other data except the primary key's value tuple are sent since the *operation transfer* mode is adopted.

Data changes should be sent by the time order of change occurrence labeled by *Timestamp*, otherwise, the sync results in the receiver side could be wrong, unless no source data record undergoes a second change, or the rightness of the receiver side's applications is independent from the change order of data.

In a non-leaf node, after changing the corresponding local data tables according to the change information received, the sync engine shall record such changes in the local *change-log* and assign *URI_origin*, *Birth_time* and *URI_sync* of the log records with appropriate information accordingly.

Table 2. Last sync-time

field	description
URI	URI of data table of sync-client
Timestamp	Last sync time (in server's clock)
Sync_pattern	Last sync pattern
Last_interval	Interval between last two syncs

As to the time baseline of each round of sync, only one end of a sync pair is required to note down the timestamp of the last sync – this is sufficient for time reference, and can be implemented by maintaining a table of *last sync-time* (see Table 2). In GSMS the start time of the last sync between a pair of nodes is recorded by the server side according to the server's clock, such a design and HS topology together make precise clock sync (between sync nodes) unnecessary. Although precise clock syncs may benefit conflict reconciliations in flexibility, however, this will increase the overhead of sync time and space.

In order to save the space overhead of *change-log*, especially regarding the limited resource of client-only devices such as PDA, cell phone, it is better to purge the *change-log*'s records that have be used successfully after each round of syncs, except for sever node where the log records should be kept until the server has synced successfully with all its sync-clients, that is, *[Purging Stipulation]:* The records of *change-log* having been successfully used for all related syncs should be purged.

According to the design principle of less intervention in higher level applications, data applications should run normally no matter any process of change propagation is going, and then concurrent issues are inevitable, such as the *ambiguous timestamp* problem: if the sync timestamp refers to the start time of sync, the data changes created during this round of sync will always be synced at the next round of sync regardless whether these changes have been synced or not in this round; if the sync timestamp refers to the end time of sync, then the data changes created during this round of sync will never be synced since these changes are labeled occurring before the last sync time. To avoid such a problem, the sync middleware should note down the start time of sync by the client clock – according to SyncML protocols the sync-client always plays a role of sync initiator, only syncs the changes that occurred before this timestamp, and should purge its used records of local *change-log* timely.

```
Repeat {
Update change-log C set C.sem = C.sem +1 where C.SeqN_change = value;
Select Max(sem) from change-log into sem_v where C.SeqN_change = value;
If sem_v <=1 then {
Update the record set where C.SeqN_change = value with new control information;
SQLok := true } else SQLok := false;
Update change-log C set C.sem = C.sem −1 where C.SeqN_change = value
} until SQLok
```

Figure 4. Dijkstra PV pseudo-codes.

To serialize concurrent processes that update the same record set of *change-log*, it is required to set up a critical section around any *update* manipulation on *change-log* to fulfill an exclusive lock in the record level, see Figure 4.

One core task of maintaining *change-log* is about how to map the primary key's value tuple of a data table that undergoes change into a set of records of *change-log*; such a mapping is called *key-mapping* here. Under the sync mechanism of "trigger + proprietary change log", each *change-log* can have a respective method of primary key mapping. In the following subsections, three methods of mapping primary key's value will be introduced.

6.2. KEY-MAPPING VIA ADDITIVE NUMBERING COLUMN

This approach is implemented by adding an integer column *row_ID* in data tables for numbering uniquely any data records and, in *change-log* let *SeqN_change* = *row_ID* to indicate the relevant change records if any. Whenever a data record is inserted or updated, it is not requested using fields *Key_field* and *StrValue_kf*, however, when a data record is deleted, each $(f_i,$ Str$(f_i))\{1{\leq}i{\leq}k\}$ must be stored in fields *Key_field* and *StrValue_kf* under different change records. Therefore, it is required that the primary key of *change-log* should be (*table_name*, *SeqN_change*) under the *unique* constraint. *row_ID* should not be assigned any semantics but requested to ensure the uniqueness, thus, it needs maintenance only for *insert* and *Delete* manipulations (assign and recall). Then it raises a *row_ID* conflict problem: after a *Delete* manipulation on a data table, since the relevant change records in *change-log* shall remain until all its syncs with neighbor nodes have finished, and during this period if reuse a *row_ID* of a previously deleted data record, then different changed data records will take up the same *row_ID* in the *change-log*. For this problem the simplest solution is to set *row_ID* in a data type of auto-incremental integer, this will avoid any value recycle for *row_ID*. Of course, after a long time of maintenance, new *row_ID* values might eventually exceed the largest integer of the hosting computer – this should be handled periodically and carefully. Some DBMSs provide auto-incremental integer fields – such as MS SQL sever and Sybase, whenever a record is inserted the value of such a field will be assigned by the DBMS, there, the maintenance of *row_ID* can be fulfilled without resorting to any alteration on applications; some DBMSs provide only the sequence of self-increment for programming, e.g., Oracle, (noticing that the physical row address should not be used in this purpose since it will be changed by any renewal or remount of DBMS); in this case the maintenance of *row_ID* is still easy as long as DBMS provides a trigger programming entry that functions as *After_insert_trriger* of Oracle or MySQL. As to general cases, if DBMSs can guarantee the ignitions of all triggers of *Insert* manipulations are sequential, this is true de facto, and then the maintenance of *row_ID* need not bother to alter any high-level data applications, the relevant pseudo-codes are showed in Figure 5.

```
/* After_Insert_Trigger */
Select Max(D.row_ID)+1 from Table D into Seqnum;
       Update Table D set D.row_ID = Seqnum
       Where D. f₁ = D.new. f₁ and ... and D. fₖ = D.new. fₖ
```

Figure 5. Numbering by the method of ANM.

The **a**dditive **n**umbering **m**ethod (ANM) has the advantage of saving log's space without involving heavy computation in triggers – sometimes no computation at all if via the facility of DBMS auto-increment integer maintenance. In addition, at the node of change source it is not required of type reversion processing for the attribute values of the primary key: in the case of Update or Insert change, a *row_ID = SeqN_chang* can be used directly to locate all attribute values in the source table; in the case of *Delete* change, the primary value tuple {Str(f_i) | 1≤i≤k} from *change-log* are used directly to form the corresponding content of <key> element for propagating a *Delete* manipulation. Despite the merits mentioned above, in consideration of the negative influence of altering the data structure of existing applications ANM should not be in the recommended list.

```
Repeat {
Select Max(C.SeqN_change) from change-log C into Seqnum
where C.table_name = "table_data";
Seqnum := (Seqnum + 1) mod MaxNumber;
Start transaction
       Insert into change-log(Table_name, SeqN_change, Key_field, StrValue_kf)
                      Values (table_data, Seqnum, "f₁", Str(a1));
       Insert into change-log(Table_name, SeqN_change, Key_field, StrValue_kf)
                      Values (table_data, Seqnum, "f₂", Str(a2));
       ... ...
       Insert into change-log(Table_name, SeqN_change, Key_field, StrValue_kf)
                      Values (table_data, Seqnum, "fₖ", Str(ak));
Rollback on Errors; } until (SQLSTATE = OK)
```

Figure 6. The Inc method (other fields' processing is omitted).

6.3. KEY-MAPPING VIA INCREMENTAL NUMBERING

The method of incremental numbering, in short IncN, demands that the primary key of *change-log* be a tuple of (*table_name*, *SeqN_change*, *key_field*). Whenever triggers capture a data record changed they will execute a procedure as in Figure 6, where the value of the data record's primary key is $value(f_1, f_2, ..., f_k) = (a1, a2, ..., ak)$.

The above processing can also be used for concurrent control: if a value of *SeqN_change* = Max(*SeqN_change*)+1 already exists in the log, which is indicated by a SQL insert error, then the next Max(*SeqN_change*)+1 value should be tried. The correctness of the above processing needs justification only for numbering the change events from the same data table. In fact, we have,

```
j:= 0;
Repeat {
Seqnum := (a1+j)×(a2+ j)×... ×(ak+ j) mod Maxnumber; /* hash(a1,a2.... ,ak.j) */
j:=j+1;
Select Count(*) from change-log C into Found Where C.SeqN_change = Seqnum;
If Found = 0 Then     /* the number is unused */
{   Start Transaction
        InsertProcess(Seqnum);    /* insert the set of the change records under Seqnum */
        Select Count(*) from change-log C into Found Where C.SeqN_change = Seqnum;
        If Found > k then {Rollback; Continue Loop;}
                        /* a concurrent process reused the number */
    Commit;
    Exit; }
/* the number has been used */
Select Count(*) from change-log C into Found where C.table_name = "table_data" and C.Key_field =
        "f₁" and StrValue_kf = Str(a1) and C.SeqN_change = Seqnum;
If Found = 0 Then Continue loop; /* it is a change record of other data records */
    ... ...
Select Count(*) from change-log C into Found where C.table_name = "table_data" and C.Key_field =
        "fₖ" and StrValue_kf = Str(ak) and C.SeqN_change = Seqnum;
If Found = 0 Then Continue loop; /* it is a change record of other data records */
Repeat { /* updating the set of change records (the primary key value of the data record is unchanged) */
    Start Transaction
    UpdateProcess(Seqnum);   /* update the set of the change records under Seqnum */
    Rollback on Errors; } until (SQLSTATE = OK) ;
Exit; }
```

Figure 7. The number reuse method.

Assertion 1. For different change events on the same data table, their *SeqN_change* values in *change-log* will be different under IncN unless *SeqN_change*≥MaxNumber. That is, *SeqN_change* increases without repetition under IncN.

Proof. Due to the uniqueness of (*table_name*, *SeqN_change*, *key_field*) of *change-log*, a SQL insert error will occur whenever a value of *SeqN_change* is reused. □

The changes from *Delete* manipulations are propagated directly in the *operation transfer* mode as mentioned before. As to the changes made by *Update* and *Insert* manipulations, a value of the primary key shall be used to locate the data records to be synced in the source table before the changes propagation start.

6.4. KEY-MAPPING VIA NUMBER REUSE

Let (*table_name*, *SeqN_change*, *key_field*, *StrValue_kf*) be the primary key of *change-log*. Whenever triggers capture a change of data record, they shall execute a procedure as described in Figure 7, called the number reuse, where the value of the data record's primary key is $value(f_1, f_2, ..., f_k) = (a1, a2, ..., ak)$. The objective of the number reuse is to reduce the number of change-log records for the same data record. If the values of $hash(a1,a2,... ,ak,0)$ are distributed ideal, much likely one data record corresponds to one change record. In fact, we can have,

Assertion 2. Under the number, reuse method: *change-log's* record sets for different data changes of the same data record identity would not be mixed, and in general, they likely have an identical *SeqN_change*. As for different data changes under different data record identities of the same data table, the corresponding sets of change records in *change-log* will have a different value of *SeqN_change*.

Proof.1) Noticing that DBMSs assure all *Update* manipulations on the same record are executed sequentially, and a trigger procedure is part of *Update* manipulation, thus, executions of trigger script will be isolated, and then regarding that the update process of the number reuse method is all-or-nothing, therefore, it is concluded that sets of change records from different data changes under the same value of the data record's primary key, would not be mixed—under the same *SeqN_change* all change records are belonged to a single data change event.

2) Due to the fine distribution of numbers produced by *hash*(a1,a2,... , ak,0), often a further hash on the primary key's value tuple is not needed, thereby, much likely the number of *SeqN_change* is set by *hash*(a1,a2,... ,ak,0) for all data changes that are with *value*($f_1, f_2, ..., f_k$) = (a1, a2, ..., ak).

3) Without losing generality, a typical concurrent case is concerned: at first *Sa* is the number of *SeqN_change* for Key*A*, a value of the data record's primary key, and then Key*A* is sharing *Sa* with Key*B*, another value of the data record's primary key, that is, at first a process that notes down the changed data record under Key*A* has inserted its *Sa* labeled change records into *change-log*, at the meantime, a concurrent process for recording the changed data record under Key*B* also runs its number reuse procedure. According to the program in Figure 7, the later finisher of Key*A* and Key*B* shall rollback certainly in this case, and then there is no sharing *Sa* of Key*A* and Key*B* anymore. Thus, the number reuse method would not allow a number of *SeqN_change* to be shared by sets of change records from different data record identities of the same data table. □

The processing of sending change information is similar to those in the previous section. The number reuse method is much complicate than the other two, and has a poor running efficiency, especially subject to programming and running environments, therefore, we do not recommend it in general.

Chapter 7

SYNC SESSIONS AND
THEIR OPTIMIZATIONS

Conforming to the asymmetry of SyncML protocols, GSMS offers four choices of sync patterns: two-way, slow, one-way, and refresh. The former two are bilateral, whereas the later two are unilateral – the refresh pattern is referred to an overlay replication in the direction from the server to client. Both the two-way and one-way patterns belong to the *incremental mode* while the others belong to the *total mode*. Hereinto, in the slow pattern a pair of sync nodes exchanges the whole contents between data replicas, whereas in the refresh pattern the replica of the sync server will overlay that of the sync-client. Normally, the refresh pattern is used in special scenarios such as restoring data in client ends, or downloading data replicas – when the client devices are taken as receiver only, which often corresponds to the case the authority of the server node is higher than that of the client nodes.

The sync sessions of *total mode* often last too long, it will increase the probability of propagation exceptions. Normally, sync patterns of *total mode* are only used for initializing sync systems. Sync processing of *total mode* is often related to special tasks of system maintenance, while in general an instance of software running in the status of maintenance should exclusively occupy its maintaining objects to shorten the maintenance time and avoid the errors caused by share use – especially for very large objects of replica. Besides, GSMS should enable a sync process be restorable from the last interrupt point – which requires adopting in advance a "try and confirm" lock-step mechanism to coordinate the propagation sessions between sync nodes.

Transferring a great amount of data in one session must be tackled carefully, which should be avoided as well, because the rushing-in data probably exceeds the web server's capacity, this results a severe decline of service performance, and even a system collapse. Such phenomena are likely encountered in sync patterns of *total mode* when processing data tables with a big amount of records, or any sync patterns when syncing a record of huge size, sometimes, they might occur as the sync web server assumes a policy of "cache-all and write-once" (an optimization measure recommended by SyncML protocols [17]) – possible cache overflows. Therefore, a big replication should be divided into several sync sessions such that each session transfers only a subset of the sync record content. Then, the performance problem finally comes down into how to handle a single sync record of huge size – can such a record be divided horizontally into smaller units to be packed into XML elements respectively [18]?

In our sync model, propagations of large data records occur only when syncing *Update* or *Insert* manipulations. To know the lower limit of propagation unit's size on the level of sync protocols, we recall the related contents of SyncML presentation protocols [16, 17]: a set of operations organized by their semantics is called a SyncML package, and each SyncML operation usually corresponds to a DML manipulation of DBMSs; typically, a SyncML package carries a group of information for the data changes made by a bundle of DML manipulations. If the packages are too big, then they should be divided into a series of SyncML message – the smallest self-contained unit propagated by SyncML sessions [18]. An *Update* DML manipulation can be substituted by a series of Update operations of which each exerts on an individual field; whereas, an *Insert* manipulation is equivalent to a *Insert* manipulation exerting only on every fields from the primary key, plus an *Insert* manipulation exerting on other fields of the relation record – if the receiver can handle well the case that the values of some non-primary fields are still unknown, e.g. such fields can be assigned a *Null* value by default or temporarily. In the open source project *sync4j* [6], a properly set value of length threshold is used for dividing big SyncML messages.

Up to now, it is known that the lower limit of a SyncML message's length equals to the length of the data record primary key plus the length of the largest field outside the primary key. Any further division of message is ascribed to the processing of lower level protocols, such as HTTP or WAP, etc.

To reduce repetitive contents of sync transmission, refining the granularity of data change record is a common method of optimization: data changes are recorded into *change-log* based on individual fields (see Table 1). However, such an approach has a constraint that, should it not assign a set of change records for each change, then there probably arises a problem:

[Scenario 1] Given that, after a new data record is inserted in node *S*, a neighbor node *C* has synced that new record with *S*, but, other neighbor nodes of *S* have not synced with *S*, and then any subsequent *Update* manipulations for partial fields on *S* cannot turn the value "N" of field *Change_type* of Table 1 into "U", otherwise, all neighbor nodes except *C* will miss syncing the values of the fields that have not been listed in *Chg_lst_fields*.

Obviously, Scenario 1 implies a redundant sync on the field level. Of course, if each data record owns just one set of change records for each change, such as that in the additive numbering column and incremental numbering methods, there will be no the problem of the scenario 1. In addition, the chance of *Chg_lst_fields* listing most of fields' names could not be neglected, thus, to save space and simplify processing, it is requested of a binary string to express uniformly the values of *Chg_lst_fields*.

There are some questions associated with the transform of sync patterns. Let us consider a transform from a bilateral sync to a unilateral replication at first: how to treat the data change that takes place just after the last bilateral sync but before the first execution of the new unilateral replication. A routine approach is that, after the configuration of sync mode is changed, the sync engine should immediately execute an additive sync in the previous mode; if such sync causes a version conflict, then it should be reconciled by GSMS in the new mode. Transformations from a bilateral sync to a unilateral replication can be addressed in a similar way but regarding that a normal unilateral replication is mandatorily overlaying – none of version conflict will arise.

Chapter 8

ENGINEERING PRINCIPLES AND CONFLICT RECONCILIATION

In the practice of developing software product, there might be too many minutiae of trade-off, which might appear incongruous even contradicted from time to time. Thus, especially for conflict reconciliation, a key design principle must be hold: solutions on a lower level of coupling with application are preferred. For easy implementations, we raise several core engineering guidelines for conflict reconciliation, which are named after Codes for Sync Engineering [3], in short CSE:

CSE 1. Avoiding unobservable sync overlays from different changes of data except those resulted from explicit rules.

CSE 2. In case of auto-processing, the version with a higher possibility of semantics priority should surpass those with a lower such possibility.

CSE 3. GSMS should provision a manual handling function.

CSE 4. Any detected conflicts should not disappear of themselves.

CSE 5. Encountering detected conflict is better than missing a data change.

CSE 6. The manual handling should be separated from the process of sync action.

Essentially CSE 2 is semantics-relevant; its syntax implementation depends statistically on the distribution of use cases. In our GSMS solution, we provide five basic auto-reconciliation rules, in short AuRC rules:

1. Jurisdiction priority.

2. Diligence priority.
3. Server wins.
4. Client wins.
5. Last-writer wins, the so-called Thomas write rule [5].

The AuRC rule 1 is applicable only when a jurisdiction table exists, see Table 3. The jurisdiction table indicates that the jurisdiction of a data object belongs to which node, or the so-called subject. The AuRC rule 3 is based on the consideration that: a client who syncs more frequently with the server is more apt to having the newest information, and by common knowledge it is more likely that the applications which change data more frequently should be configured as syncing more frequently with the sever in order to propagate new changes in time. If the interval between the last two syncs is used to measure the frequency of sync, then a concrete implementation of AuRC rule 2 is gotten – "the last shorter interval wins". The rest of the rules are self-explanatory.

Table 3. An example of a jurisdiction table

Seq	Table name	SQL-relation expression	Subject's URI	URI type	Subject name
1	*data_table1*	String(address,1,4) = "4401"	202.155.23.98	IP	Company A
2	*data_table2*	String(address,1,4) = "4402"	133XXX12345	Phone Number	Mr. W
...	...	...	...	...	...

The main aim of using auto-reconciliation is to avoid manually intervening in applications on higher levels, this is extremely important for data sync infrastructure. However, no AuRC rules can get rid of abnormal exceptions, even for the most reliable AuRC rule 1 there is still a bad case: a conflict occurs when a data update made by the subject is wrong while other nodes are correcting their data replicas. In general, it is advised to apply the AuRC rule 1 preferentially, other rules then come by the list order – but it should also be based on the factors emphasized on: whether the responsibility or the freshness of data comes first, the former shall choose AuRC rule 3 or 4, the later shall select AuRC rule 2 or 5.

Although a versatile mechanism of conflict auto-reconciliation is unavailable, it is still possible to offer a conflict auto-reconciliation method aiming at certain typical domains of applications under AuRC rule 1 – this semantics-relevant approach might encounter exceptions too, actually is of partial auto-handling, named the Jurisdiction table method, whose concrete design is as follows:

1. Configure a jurisdiction table at the server side such that, each record of the table is used to designate which record of a specific data table is under the jurisdiction of what node – the **subject** (see Table 3). When handling a sync conflict, GSMS will locate a judge record for the conflicted data table in the jurisdiction table – using the subject's URI (Universal Resource Identity) to search; if a judge record is matched, its SQL-relation expression will be calculated – if true, then the subject marked by the judge record is designated as the winner in the conflict.

2. The method described in (1) can be used jointly with the rule of server wins or client wins: applying the jurisdiction table method first, if no rules from the jurisdiction table are applicable – no record matched or the matched record's SQL-relation expression takes a "false" vale, and then applying the other rules.

Caution is required for conflict auto-reconciliation, since rules are fixed but contexts are variable, the results of applying different rules might be equivalent or widely divergent, that is, the sync administrator should choose appropriate rules and decide their priorities basing on application scenarios. For example, if the last writer comes from a node that syncs with the server in a lower frequency and likely has updated the data replica thereof with a dated version, then "the last shorter interval wins" instead of Thomas write rule should be assumed. Sometimes a phenomenon of "earlier writer wins" could arise from the application of AuRC rule 2: suppose both client A and B have updated respectively their replica of the same data object, the update of client B is later than that of client A; since the interval of client A's syncs with the server is shorter, client A transfers its update to the server certainly earlier than Client B, and according to rule 2, the earlier update from client A will defeat the later update from client B no matter which is fresher.

In applying the rule of "server wins", two typical cases should be considered here: 1) the server version of data replica might come from the server itself, or 2) possibly from a client that previously synced with the server. In quite a number of cases, "server wins" is equivalent to "the last shorter interval wins", such as Figure 8 shows: given that, the interval of client A's bilateral syncs is shorter than that of client B's, both client A and client B

start their syncs from the baseline of the same last shared version of data object O_1, and when client B propagates its update of O_1 to the server, there will occur an update conflict. If the "server wins" rule is applied, since the client A's update has become the new O_1 version of the server, and then the client A is actually the winner, this result is as the same as "the last shorter interval wins" rule is used. However, there is a contrary result, which is shown in Figure 9.

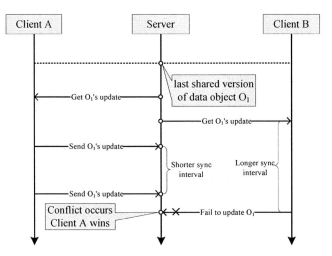

Figure 8. Conflict scenario A.

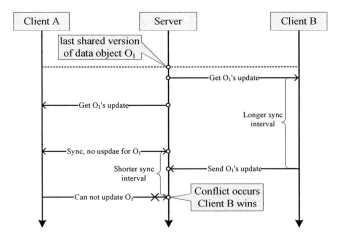

Figure 9. Conflict scenario B.

The last resort for conflict reconciliation relies on manual handling, which is indispensable – GSMS must provide. The fundamental functions of manual handling are outlined as follows,

(1) Each side of the conflict preserves their own version, only the server node needs to maintain the detect record of conflict– (*conflict_seq_num, Client URI, data table name, primary key, detect time, status*), if there is no such a record, then the next round of sync will go against the CSE 4.

(2) The software module of manual handling should show in its GUI every pair of conflicted records to the user, and offers the following basic selections:

    (a) Keeping one of the pair of conflicted data records;

    (b) Create a new data record to replace the pair of conflicted data records;

    (c) Both records of the conflicted record pair are kept locally if they are equivalent in semantics, and then the detect record of conflict is deleted.

(3) Cutting down side effects of conflict reconciliation – by exclusive use of record set: handling record pairs conflicted serially. By means of semaphore processing, each time only one running process of conflict reconciliation is permitted to use the record table of conflict detect.

(4) If the result of conflict reconciliation is to write a data record in the database of the client or server side, then,

    (a) GSMS implements the writing of data records;

    (b) GSMS notes down the data changes directly in *change-log*, which would not ignite the triggers; otherwise, there would be a vibration phenomenon of iterative syncs for the same data change.

    (c) Deleting the corresponding detect records of conflict.

Besides, if a client seldom uploads its update, then some kind of optimistic approach could be used to suppress the conflict questions related to such a client [5].

Chapter 9

PERFORMANCE AND
RELIABILITY ISSUES

There are two major negative influences worthy of consideration: 1) aggravating load; 2) increasing errors or exceptions – those can be captured and tolerated by DBMS.

To lessen the burden of the node where GSMS resides, the first thing is to relieve the burden of auto-mechanism, and the second is to plan well the configuration of sync tasks. The former is correlated to the change-capture triggers since they are used most frequently and located in the deepest core of the GSMS inner part, the latter is mainly associated to the sync frequency and topology. The following intuitive measures are suggested for relieving burden: simplifying trigger scripts as possible, handing over sophisticated processing to the outer part of GSMS – e.g. replaced by outer polling programs, etc; under the satisfaction of time precondition, it had better decrease sync frequency and ensure that sync topology contains no loop of path.

As to the problems of exceptions, the robustness of triggers is the main concern. In general, the running errors of a well-designed DBMS product mostly come from the concurrent writing to the same data record. Typical scenarios of exceptions are as these: let p_k is a value of the primary key of a data table, an exception will occur when 1) a data record indicated by p_k is inserted if another process has inserted a data record with a primary key's value equal to p_k; or when 2) a data record indicated by p_k is updated if that data record has been deleted by another concurrent process. Of course, such scenarios can be avoided by using a system lock on table level, however, which if used frequently would seriously deteriorate the performance of related applications, especially is not suitable for already busy systems. Here we would rather spend more on the processing of error captures to reduce application abort events.

As to the propagation performance of GSMS, since sync information exchange is based on XML, it is crucial to raise the speed of packing change records into XML documents and restoring them from XML documents back to records of RDBMS. Besides, the format design of field *chg_lst_fields* of *change-log* can also influence the performance of GSMS. If the content of column *chg_lst_fields* is expressed in the form of string of field names, suppose that the average length of names is L, and the list contains at most M fields' names, then the upper limit of the space used by that column is $L*M$ bytes, whereas it requests only $M/8$ bytes for a string expression of binary bits. Although the string expression of binary bits is rather simple (see Figure 10), it requires a special mapping table that maps the names of fields onto the bits or in return the bits back to the names of fields, this may have an overhead which cannot be neglected with respect to the triggers running. According to our practices, however, the degradation of processing speed is not significant if the mapping table is placed in the same RDBMS instead of a XML file.

Integer M;
1) Check if the n-th bit of M's binary expression is 1:
    $Chk(n,M) = ((M \bmod 2^n) / 2^{(n-1)} == 1)$
2) Set the n-th bit of M's binary expression to 1:
    If not(Chk(n,M)) $M = M + 2^{(n-1)}$
3) Clear the n-th bit of M's binary expression to 0:
    If (Chk(n,M)) $M = M - 2^{(n-1)}$

Figure 10. Pseudo-codes for bit manipulations inside trigger.

In addition, the sync configuration can be optimized according to the running performance of GSMS. As for this, several evaluation indices are introduced, such as, 1) *Miss-span*–how many times of data changes the replica have encountered between two subsequent sync actions; 2) *Propagation-span* – the time interval between two subsequent sync actions, its reciprocal is the *sync frequency*; etc. Then sync configurations might be improved via sampling analysis on the values of such indices.

Furthermore, the best measure of optimizing sync propagation should be that, jointly applying the "self-adaptive horizontal partition" mechanism to adapt for nodes' sync capacities, and adopting the "resuming propagation at stop points" method to build up an auto- or manual- restoration mechanism [30], regarding the problems of instability and low availability due to poor transmission condition and sync capacity.

Chapter 10

CORRECTNESS OF
MULTIPLE TABLE SYNC

In RDBMS applications, the data semantics could appear in the form of constraints across tables, of which perhaps the most typical is the foreign key constraint, in short FKC, e.g. a teacher code in the *curriculum schedule* table should appear in the *faculty* table as its primary key. Given that, node A and B should sync with each other; if $FKC(A) \subseteq FKC(B)$, then the content of data changes having synced completely from node B will satisfy the FKC in node A, but it is not true vice versa. However, as to the propagation pattern of *operation transfer mode*, even for the $B \rightarrow A$ sync there are still exceptions: if the sequence of operations is not carried out in the right order, such as, deleting the teacher code of the *faculty* table first, and then deleting the records labeled by that code in the *curriculum schedule* table – this is a typical problem in multiple table syncs. Of course, if a data record is not involved in any relation across multiple tables, then its sync is still treated as single table sync; otherwise, further considerations are needed:

- *As to "timed sync" and "manual sync" modes, if the related data applications (that are sharing the data with GSMS) are well-designed, e.g. the correlated updates are completed within in a single transaction, then the data objects to be synced that are resulted from these applications belong to the consistent data change set. There it requires only that the correlated data change syncs be fulfilled within a single transaction. But, the question is how can we know which records of data changes belong to the same transaction? – it is very hard to reflect a transaction of client data applications in change-log.*

- *As to "real-time sync" mode, in which the sync process should be ignited instantly by data change, the change propagation will be postponed until all correlated changes are entirely completed – whether this is feasible or not depends on the concrete implementation of the real-time sync. If the approach uses a polling method, e.g., polling on change-log, which is written by triggers, the question finally comes down to how to judge which records created early or late in change-log whether belong to the same transaction or not – which is application-specific.*

In sum, if applications on higher levels do not cooperate or learn all these cases – which cannot be enumerated in advance, to entirely handle the correlated data records is impossible. However, as to DBMS built-in constraints, e.g. foreign key constraints, could it be disposed properly? Suppose, a proposition *real_ref* = "the result that DML triggers write *change-log* really reflects a practical process allowed by DBMS (all its constraints including those cross tables are met)" is true, then the succeeding sync actions will eventually sync all correlated data changes together into the target systems, and the possible inconsistency between replicas of the synced node pair is temporary at most – provided such sync renewals are accepted by all target systems. Of course, a precondition is assumed: *constraint*(Souce) $\supseteq$ *constraint*(Target), which should be verified at the sync configuration stage. Temporary inconsistent phenomena must be tolerated and eventually eliminated in distributed data syncs. Obviously, if no exceptions occur in any data applications, then the preposition *real_ref* is certainly true. Thus, regarding the correctness of multiple table syncs in GSMS, we need only consider the following cases where data applications under the protection of transaction throw exceptions:

1. An execution of a trigger aborts.
2. An execution of a SQL statement aborts.
3. A DBMS stored procedure aborts.
4. A hosting program that calls DBMS operations or stored procedures, aborts.

The reason for the above-mentioned cases aiming at "abort" phenomenon is based on the fact: if an instruction encapsulation body (a trigger script, SQL statement, DBMS stored procedure, procedure of high level program language) throws an exception, then such an exception could only be captured and handled outside the encapsulation body meanwhile the execution of the encapsulation body shall abort. As to case (1), the DML in which the trigger resides will be roll-backed as the trigger aborts – this is true for all current mainstream RDBMS products (no matter whether "trigger after DML" or "trigger before DML" is set), and if all write operations of the trigger (including its write exerting on *change-log*) are brought into a transaction – they will be rollbacked together due to the abort, then the issue of "*real_ref* is true" will go up to case (2)—no write effect remains on the current level, only an exception is thrown upwards to the higher level hosting encapsulation body. As to case (2), since today mainstream RDBMS products can ensure: "whenever a SQL operation aborts, its attached triggers of DML level will be roll-backed at the same time", thereby, similarly the issue of "*real_ref* is true" will go up to case (3) or (4), regarding the higher level encapsulation hosting body. As for the case (3), if all write operations of the stored procedure are brought into a transaction, then DBMS will rollback all these write operations together, and the issue of "*real_ref* is true" will go up to case (4) similarly. As to case (4), if the hosting program has all its write operations protected under a transaction, then it can erase the effect made by already executed DMLs as in a whole after an abort occurs by measures of rollback or compensation. If assuming the measures mentioned above, the execution series of all write operations from an application will eventually produce a consistent data result since all write operations are fulfilled via executing DBMS DMLs.

[Notice] a rollback is a reverse operation for a specific operation, which takes place before the transaction is committed, thus its result is invisible for the outsiders of the transaction; while compensation happens after the transaction commits, which uses a reverse measure to erase or reverse the effect of a specific operation. Normally, under the protection scope of transaction of RDBMS products, the effects of operations, which are carried out before the transaction commits, are restrained in the memory space, and are not written into the persistent storage; thus, they can be erased upon a roll-back.

Chapter 11

INEQUITABLE SYNC

In the database applications of distributed autonomous cooperations, the feasibility of data sync requires that sync nodes should have in common a comprehension of the semantics of the minimum data item, i.e. field. Nevertheless, necessary considerations for mapping relation should certainly go beyond the field lay, for example:

[Example 1] Given that, relation tables $A(\text{key}, a_1,a_2,...,a_m)$, $B(\text{key},b_1,b_2,...,b_n)$, and $C(\text{key},a_1,a_2,...,a_k,b_1,...,b_j)$, which belong to DBMS in different nodes respectively, and data sync $(A,B) \rightarrow C$ is required. Obviously, the equitable reverse sync $C \rightarrow (A,B)$ may not exist, in other words, $(A,B) \rightarrow C$ is an inequitable sync.

This is a scenario of the so-called inequitable sync. To the best of our knowledge, today existent data sync systems in general fall in short of inequitable sync disposal function. First, a clear definition should be given before further investigation:

Definition 1. An inequitable sync is referred to a unilateral sync: $\mathfrak{S} \rightarrow$, where R is a relation, $\mathfrak{S}$ is a set of relation, and the relations of $\mathfrak{S}$ might come from different nodes, $R = \mathfrak{S}$, $\varphi \mathfrak{S}$ is a relational expression of $\mathfrak{S}$, which uses operators only from $\{ \cup ,-, \times, \pi, \sigma \}$, that is, the set of relational operator "and", "difference", "Cartesian product", "project", and "selection". □

Aiming at this definition, we raise the following sync algorithm:

[Algorithm 1] A sync mapping of field granularity for all local data tables that should receive changes is uniformly defined as in table 4.

Table 4. Data table sync mapping

Name of sync table	Sync attribute	Corresponding remote sync attribute
T	a_1	$Node_1.database_1.table_1.attri\_name_1$
...	...	...
P	a_q	$Node_q.database_q.table_q.attri\_name_q$

Meanwhile a sync scope table for each local database is set:

Change_depend_rel(localtablename, sync_table_URI)

Here, all kinds of data changes shall be propagated by the content transfer mode. At receiving a sync data record X, the local sync engine uses $S(X)$, the name of source table of X, to match *sync_table_URI* of *Change_depend_rel* in order to locate

Target:= localtablename(sync_table_URI= =S(X)).

And then,

1. If the data change is made by a *Delete* operation, the arriving record X shall be regarded as the whole data tuples of $S(X)$ for calculating $\varphi \; \ominus$ to create the data set $\varphi \; \ominus \; |X$, afterward all records of $\varphi \; \ominus \; |X$ should be deleted from the current set of data records of R.

2. If the data change is made by an *Insert* operation, the arriving record X shall be regarded as the whole data tuples of $S(X)$ for calculating $\varphi \; \ominus$ to create the data set $\varphi \; \ominus \; |X$, afterward all records of $\varphi \; \ominus \; |X$ should be inserted into the current set of data records of R.

3. If the data change is made by an *Update* operation, key(X) shall be used to locate the corresponding data records in *Target* to update the value of each matched local attribute with the content of X according to the mapping relation defined by Table 4. □

Before further investigation, let us considering an inequitable sync scenario of Definition 1:

[Scenario 1]

Relational R_1 belongs to node N1, its initial data table is

OwnerID	OwnerName	CarType	YearMade
00001	J. smith	Fox 00A	2002
00002	M. Lord	CruiserX	2008
00003	H. Wang	Jet99	2009

Relational R_2 belongs to node N2, its initial data table is

VendorID	Cartype	CarAmout	YearMade
C0001	Fox 00A	1000	2001
C0002	CruiserX	3000	2008
C0003	Jet99	999	2009

There are two inequitable syncs mapping data to Node N3:

1) $\mathfrak{S} = \{R_1, R_2\}$, $R = \varphi$ $\mathfrak{S}$ = SELECT * FROM R_1 WHERE *YearMade* < 2003

2) $\mathfrak{S} = \{R_1, R_2\}$, $R = \varphi$ $\mathfrak{S}$ = SELECT R_1.*, R_2.*OwnerID* FROM R_1, R_2 WHERE R_1.*CarType*=R_2.*CarType* and R_1.*YearMade*=R_2.*YearMade*

Then, $R = \varphi$ $\mathfrak{S}$ has its data table of first sync:

OwnerID	OwnerName	CarType	YearMade
00001	J. smith	Fox 00A	2002

While $R = \varphi$ $\mathfrak{S}$ has its data table of first sync:

OwnerID	VendorID	OwnerName	CarType	YearMade
00001	C0001	J. smith	Fox 00A	2002
00002	C0002	M. Lord	CruiserX	2008
00003	C0003	H. Wang	Jet99	2009

Afterward, J. smith's car was ruined by an accident, and he bought a new car of the same type, the new card was manufactured in the year 2006. As a result, the first data record of R_1 should be updated by Set *YearMade*=2006. Therefore, if the result of the second sync is correct, then the data table of φ $\mathfrak{S}$ will be empty (no data record is selected), while the data table of φ $\mathfrak{S}$ after a new round of sync:

OwnerID	VendorID	OwnerName	CarType	YearMade
00002	C0002	M. Lord	CruiserX	2008
00003	C0003	H. Wang	Jet99	2009

The above examples show that each sync action for an *Update* change might result a delete (or insert) effect. Now a question arises: likely an inequitable sync action needs calculating $\varphi\,\mathfrak{S}$ to rebuild the data table for the target relation (in order to ensure all data of R are still the result of calculating $\varphi\,\mathfrak{S}$), i.e., resetting a target table. If so, its expense could be very high, and then instead if allowable we would rather utilize more space to save time: build locally all data tables (must be synced) for relations of $\mathfrak{S}$, and then create a view equitable to R on these local tables. As for the question "in what circumstance no resetting is required for an inequitable sync caused by *Update* change?" we have,

Assertion 3. As to the inequitable sync $\mathfrak{S}\rightarrow$ defined by Definition 1, if

$$(\forall\quad\in\mathfrak{S}\;\exists\qquad\in\qquad\quad\ni(R)\},$$

i.e., for any relation in $\mathfrak{S}$ there exists a key, of which all attributes belong to the attribute set of relation R, and then, as for a *Update* changes of $\mathfrak{S}$, which do not increase or decrease the records resulted from calculating $\varphi\,\mathfrak{S}$ before the change, the execution of Algorithm 1 needs no resetting the sync data table of R provided that no primary key value of any source data record is changed.

Proof. Whenever a data record of any source relation S has changed its value, the data change is indicated by key(S), Algorithm 1 can use key(S) to locate the corresponding data record set in the data table of relation R, thereby GSMS can make the data update on the target table. □

Assertion 4. As to the inequitable sync $\mathfrak{S}\rightarrow$ defined by Definition 1, if

$$(\forall S\in\mathfrak{S}\;\exists\,k_s\qquad S\;\wedge k_s\in\qquad R\;\wedge$$
$$\exists A\in\qquad S\;\cap\qquad R\;\wedge A\notin k_s$$

and relation R is 3NF [26], and then, as for a *Update* changes of $\mathfrak{S}$, which do not increase or decrease the records resulted from calculating $\varphi\,\mathfrak{S}$ before the change, in the case when any R's attribute not from its primary key can have a null value, the sync data table of R needs no resetting for the executions of Algorithm 1.

Proof. Regarding $(\forall\quad\in\mathfrak{S}\;\exists\qquad\wedge\quad\in\qquad(R)\}$, we first prove that k_s is also a key of R: otherwise, from

$\exists$ $\in$ $\cap$ $\land$ $\notin$, it is derived that $k_s \rightarrow$ is a partial or transitive dependency in R, this is contrary to that R is 3NF [27]. Thereby, any change made by *Delete*(k_s) operations from the change source $\mathfrak{S}$ will be implemented in the target relation R, so will any change made by *Insert*(k_s) since the attributes of R which are outside R's primary key can have a null value. As to *Update* change that alters the primary key's value, considering that $Update(key_{old} \rightarrow$ $) = <Delete(key_{old}),\ Insert(key_{new}$ $)>$, thus we got the assertion proved.

In practical applications, corresponding to the asymmetry of SyncML protocols, the sync-mapping table is in general supplied in the server side, accordingly, the receiver of inequitable sync is normally located in the server side – any node could be configured as a server only if it can provide web services.

Chapter 12

SYNC NETWORK [3]

From the view of each data replica, a running sync process appears as an ongoing progress with a series of save points in the way, thus, a sync transaction can be also regarded as "distributed progressive version-merging transaction", in short DPVT. Each "save point" corresponds to a version-merging node where different versions of a replica meet. As to DPVT, a series of snapshots that display many intermediate statuses of a replica reflects the change history that the replica has experienced.

Up to now, we have not investigated the influence that the sync topology exerts on the target of eventual consistency of sync data replicas. To this end, we will discuss the issue of successful DPVT implementation from the viewpoint of sync network. Let us clarify several basic concepts first:

- ***Unilateral policy of conflict reconciliation*** – *Sync nodes can autonomously define their local consistent replicas whenever encountering a conflict.*
- ***Peer reconciliation of conflict*** – *Both sides of a sync pair adopt the unilateral policy of conflict reconciliation.*
- ***Sync graph*** – *the trace that sync-waves traverse, which consists of the following parts:*

1. Node – the hosting DBMS where the replicas reside.
2. Directed edge – each connects a pair of nodes, which indicates a unilateral propagation of data change along the direction of the directed edge.

3. Undirected edge – each connects a pair of nodes, which indicates a bilateral propagation of data change between the two nodes of the connected pair.

4. Arrow, i.e., a degraded directed edge – the tail end of a directed edge is deleted, which only indicates the pointed node is a change source.

- ***Oblivious sync action*** *– the receiver of sync-waves only uses the newest version of data replica to update the local replica, does not note down the origin information of the sync-wave – from which node a sync-wave is generated and at what time. Although attached version information can be used to distinguish origins of different sync-waves, it is not practical since as the data granularity becomes larger it might result in much more pseudo conflictions, and as the data granularity becomes smaller, it could cause severer storage overhead. Besides, the usage and maintenance of version label is not an easy thing regarding that any distributed data sources might create their new versions at their own will [28]. In a sync graph, an edge that an oblivious sync action correlates is called* ***oblivious edge***.

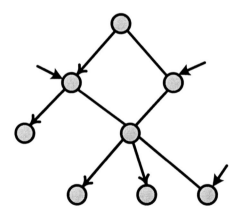

Figure 11. Sync graph.

Apparently, a *sync-graph* is a kind of *hybrid graph* – neither an undirected graph nor a pure directed graph, see Figure 11. If a sync graph does not contain a simple loop of length 3 and more, it is referred to as *acyclic* – regarding that, an undirected edge is equivalent to two opposite direction edges connecting the same pair of nodes. Then we have,

Lemma 1. Conflict can only occur at nodes with in-degree greater than 1.

Theorem 1. If a sync graph contains a directed loop of length greater than 2, and that loop at least contains an oblivious sync edge, then the corresponding sync process of the sync graph may suffer retroversion, even worse the progressive consistency may become impossible.

Proof. Considering that 1) when a sync-wave passes an oblivious edge, whose origin information is discarded and it will be regarded as a new sync-wave to be passed on; and 2) the sync-wave will refresh all synced replica along its path with its data version. Suppose B is a head node of an oblivious edge e of a directed cycle in the sync graph, and e is located in the trace of sync-wave s_w, then despite B itself as a source of data change has updated its replica to the newest version, a new arrival of s_w at B will override the real newest version of B with the stale one of s_w. As such the same sync-wave moves around the cycle, no eventual consistency will be reached.

Intuitively we call the above-described retroversion phenomenon the *circuit surge*.

Corollary 1: To ensure the eventual consistency, sync-wave traces should be acyclic.

The above discussion elucidates that an oblivious edge is permitted for the sync topology of trees only, which suggests a spanning tree of the network graph be selected as the **HS** topology to get rid of any *circuit surge*. Next, we further discuss the spanning tree issue of **HS** topology.

Tree topology itself does not divide its nodes into layers, to build hierarchy it needs defining a root for the tree, i.e. designating a node as the root. In the **HS** construction, it also requires labeling those nodes, which can only be configured as client, as leaf nodes. A leaf node has an in-degree of one, i.e. there is only one edge or arrow incisive to the node. Besides, according to the sync graph definition, there is no node with a zero in-degree.

The distributed computing model for selecting a spanning tree deserves much consideration. Referring to literature [29], we list several typical considerations with respect to **HS** spanning tree as follows:

1. *Low diameter spanning tree* is for reducing total propagation time of replica changes.
2. *Minimal-weight spanning tree* is assumed for lowering the total cost of sync along the edge set – given that each edge's weight is known.
3. *Restricted-degree spanning tree*, in which the number of edges (including arrows) attached to the same node should be controlled under a threshold value, is to limit the computation complexity,

balance workloads among server nodes, and lower the risk of conflicts.

4. *Depth-first search tree* is recommended for its easy construction, as well as for it enables nodes-labeling more convenient along its construction process – nodes-labeling is a basis of distributed computing.

Chapter 13

CONCURRENT CONTROL

Sync is a typical distributed computing in nature, it could not avoid the issue of concurrently accessing shared data resources. To ensure components of GSMS work rightly, executions of critical section codes of concurrent programs must be isolated, which will eventually resort to a locking mechanism – it probably causes some bad side effects, e.g. degradation of DBMS performance, and dead locks due to abnormal pending or aborting.

Because the change log is separated from data tables, to turn down the possibility of missing a single capture of data changes, GSMS should lock the related records in the sync data tables and *change-log* during the entire interval of each sync activity. If client applications are well designed for concurrent processing, they should at least "write-lock" all critical data records, and be ready for capturing any exception relating to accessing these records. On the level of DML manipulation, in general, the attached triggers are regarded as a partial content of the hosting DML operation, and embedding a trigger script into a DML operation does not influence the isolation or atomicity of the original DML operation. However, such embedding would increase the risk of encountering a dead lock. Therefore, we should write specific unlocking scripts to tackle dead locks caused by exceptions instead of restarting DBMS – which should be the final resort.

While using record level locks, the phantom lock phenomenon seems needing attention: locking a deleted record. Such a scenario might occur when: a client process is deleting a data record $r1$ – this DML operation ignites a trigger for change-capture to update a corresponding record $r2$ in *change-log*, and meanwhile a concurrent sync process (which has locked $r2$) has to lock $r1$ in order to implement the data renewal on $r1$ according to $r2$. Nevertheless, this *Delete* transaction could not be committed before the sync process completes since in the same DBMS a DML operation together and its trigger procedures are treated as an atomic procedure, therefore, the concurrent sync process will accomplish the data renewal on $r1$ – the phantom lock phenomenon is inexistent, there exists only lock exceptions (including dead lock).

There is a concurrent issue, which is related to that a sync client normally purges its stale sync logs each time as its sync process finishes: probably mistakenly deleting a log record that is newly inserted when the sync process is ongoing. To avoid such a problem, a sync process should at the sync start moment note down the clock's value, only sync those change records that have a timestamp smaller than the sync start time, and at the end of the sync process delete only the corresponding log records.

Besides, if the sync client can only configure a light-weighted DBMS without a lock mechanism, to be simple, it is suggested to adopt the so-called optimistic sync approach [5] – it is fine for the case the client end rarely propagates its data changes on its own initiative.

Chapter 14

MOBILE ACCESS

A mobile client should always remember its last synced server. If the client's update on the previous server *ps* has not been propagated to the current server *cs*, the client should ignite a new sync-wave from *ps* to *cs* (normally through an *EXEC* command element in a SyncML message), which is referred to as a MiTS (Motion ignited Third-sync). A MiTS may be guided through a frond of **HS** tree, which is referred to as a frond-MiTS. A frond-MiTS may breach the **HS** topology temporarily. Seemingly, when a MiTS has a trace of length greater than 1, which is named *indirect* MiTS, there is an option of deleting the edge that connects node to the parent node of *ps*, and replaces it with the frond connecting *ps* to *cs*, such that the sync graph is still of **HS** type. However, this approach may involve a lot of complex work, including a topology change's notice to every node that should be informed, and the initialization task for this new relatively fixed sync relation. Though the initialization task would be much easier if we set the sync baseline at the time the sync pair first connects each other, so that subsequent incremental syncs need not consider those changes that occur before the baseline, which, however, implies to forget the previous diversity including the recent changes already uploaded by the client to its former server.

To this point, we shall recall the design of server node that all received sync-waves together with their origin information are recorded in *change-log* with their arrival timestamp, and the last sync time is also kept for each ever synced neighbor node. This enables the upper tier server exchange the data changes that satisfy the time condition, only with specific intermediate nodes on a lower tier. As for an *indirect* MiTS, such processing is applicable only when no changes from other sources have ever overridden the data that the mobile client has just uploaded – normally this is true in a well-designed mobile user information application (if subject to Date's 5th rule: data fragmentation transparency), where each client has their sync proprietary data fragmentation – the projections of specific data records, and clients can only sync data within these fragmentations respectively. In general, for an indirect MiTS, both end nodes must be aware of the directions of the path connecting them in the **HS** tree – this may involve very complex sensor network algorithms [29], i.e. they need to know their next hop nodes towards each other, and recall when they synced with them the last time; otherwise, they would not be able to exchange only those changes that are not yet passed towards each other.

Chapter 15

EXPERIMENT AND TEST

Metrics for evaluating a sync product are mainly classified on three types: function, adaptation, and performance. The first two types of evaluation are relatively simple, in most of cases they are an issue of instant judgment; whereas the evaluation of performance is rather sophisticated: as for data sync, we mainly concern two aspects, one is the stability, and the other is speed. The sync speed requirement is relative and application-based, different application tasks may have different demands for sync speed, and to a great extent the sync speed is also influenced by sync data amount, Internet access status, as well as the hardware and software configuration of sync nodes, etc.; thus, only after excluding these factors can we figure out the merits or demerit of sync software design and programming implementation.

In comparison, the requirement of stability of performance for sync products intended for various environments is more universal. Thus, in respect of performance evaluation, we mainly concern with the performance stability of GSMS. Of course, it would be more comprehensive to compare GSMS with con-generic or similar products of heterogeneous data sync. Considering that commercial products for heterogeneous data sync are often very expensive, and they usually demand a high-level hardware configuration, it is unfair to compare them with the low-cost-aimed GSMS, which is especially attended for small or medium enterprise applications, to elucidate the merit or demerit of product design. So here, only the Sync4j sync system from an open source project is compared with our GSMS for testing the sync speed and stability.

15.1. PERFORMANCE AND STABILITY TEST

To test the performance and stability of GSMS, we design the following experiments: 1) comparing sync time consumptions among distributed heterogeneous DBMS sync and distributed homogeneous DBMS sync; 2) testing the fluctuation of sync time consumption on different record lengths for given distributed heterogeneous DBMS sync; and 3) investigating the relation of between the sync time and the number of sync records while doing 1) and 2).

1. Test under symmetric configurations

Suppose that node A and B sync with each other, there are two different sync configurations – one is A being the server and B being the client, and the other, B being the server while A being the client. We intend to see whether these two sync configurations make an obvious difference on GSMS sync performance or not. In order to observe if there is a significant asymmetry of GSMS sync performance, we deploy a pair of sync nodes with the same configuration: Windows XP, Pentium 4 (2.66 GHz) CPU, and 1G Memory. Then we test GSMS performance for different pair combinations of DBMS Oracle 9i and SQL server 2000, and show the experiment results in Figure 12, 13, and 14. In the diagrams and hereafter, label (S) and (C) indicate that the labeled DBMS is configured as the server or client respectively.

The test results reveal that:

a. The difference between the sync time of heterogeneous DBMSs and that of homogenous DBMSs is in general not significant, and the incremental trends of their sync time remain analogous as sync load increases, see Figure 12.
b. The sync time is approximately linear to the number of sync data records, see Figures 12, 13, and 14.
c. The sync performance of GSMS has no apparent asymmetry, see Figures 12, 13, and 14.

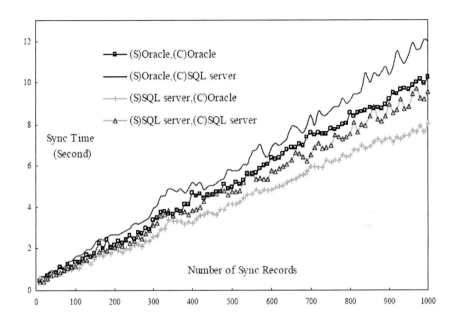

Figure 12. Comparison between homogenous and heterogeneous sync time [3].

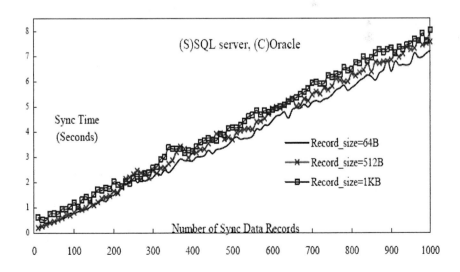

Figure 13. Sync time for different lengths of data records (heterogeneous combination A) [3].

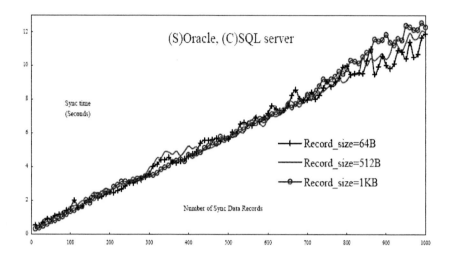

Figure 14. Sync time for different lengths of data records (heterogeneous combination B).

2. Test in a practical environment

To observe the performance and stability of GSMS in a practical environment, we test all pair combinations of Oracle 9i, SQL server 2000, and Sybase ASE12.5 in the environment of Guangdong Construction Information Center (GDCIC), where, related configurations are listed in Table 5 and 6. Remind that, the data-node where a DBMS resides is not necessarily coincided with the sync-node where a sync end is hosted. The test results are drawn in Figure 15 to 23. These test results elucidates that the sync time will increase as the number or the length of sync records increases, and as to a fixed length of data records, the sync time is basically linear to the number of sync records and the changes of the data record length do not breach such rough linear relations. These indicate that the sync performance of GSMS is rather stable.

Table 5. Hardware Configuration

Configuration	IP address	Usage
CPU: 2.0GHZ; Memory: 2.0GB; HD: 320GB	192.168.0.44	Server Node
CPU: 1.6GHZ; Memory: 1.0GB; HD: 80GB	192.168.0.46	Client Node
CPU: 1.6GHZ: Memory: 1.0GB; HD: 80GB	192.168.0.201	DBMS Node
CPU: 2.0GHZ; Memory: 1.0GB; HD: 80GB	211.155.23.98	Server Node

CPU: 2.0GHZ; Memory: 2.0GB; HD: 80GB	211.155.23.132	DBMS Node

Table 6. Software Configuration List

Name	Version	Usage
Windows	XP SP2	OS for GSMS client or sever end
Linux	RHEL AS5	OS for GSMS sever end
Linux	RedhatLinux 7.3	OS for GSMS sever end
Linux	RHEL AS3	OS for DBMS of GSMS client
Linux	RHEL AS4	OS for DBMS of GSMS sever
SQL Server	2000 SP3	DBMS
Oracle	9i	DBMS
Sybase	ASE 12.5	DBMS
Tomcat	5.0	Web server
SyncBundle	1.0	GSMS sever
SyncClient	1.0	GSMS client

Nevertheless, these test results do reflect some questions, such as, in the scenario of Sybase being deployed as the DBMS of the server end, there are some fluctuation phenomena for sync time as the number of changed data records augments in a sync session. We ascribe such fluctuation phenomena to the low configuration of the computer the Sybase server resides on, because DBMS need to frequently interchange data between the memory and the hard disk–while sync load is increasing if encountering a data swap between the memory and the hard disk, or high priority DBMS system tasks contesting for resources, GSMS sync performance would drop rapidly. Besides, regarding the performance stability, de facto Sybase is relatively a bit weaker than Oracle and MS SQL Server. Of course, the sync performance of GSMS is still quite stable for homogeneous sync tests of Sybase.

In sum, these tests make clear that the GSMS middleware that we developed has a stable sync performance: its reaction to sync load is smooth, and sync time for routine sync loads is basically controlled under the accepted level of applications.

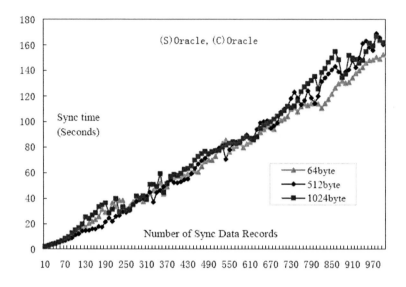

Figure 15. Performance stability test–Combination 01.

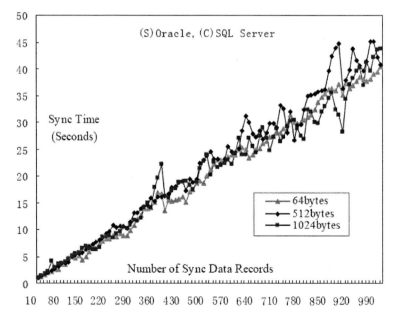

Figure 16. Performance stability test–Combination 02.

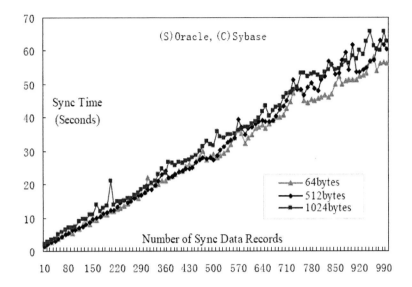

Figure 17.Performance stability test–Combination 03.

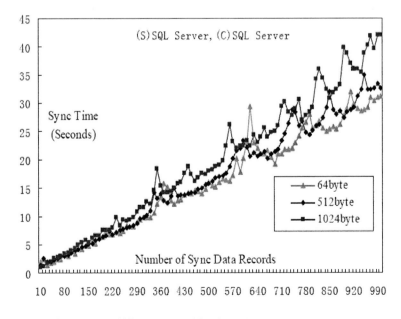

Figure 18. Performance stability test–Combination 04.

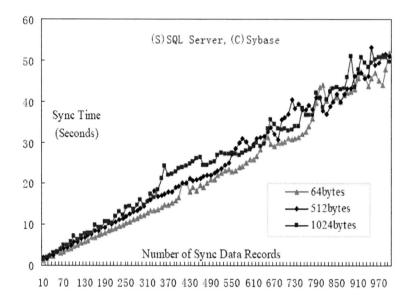

Figure 19. Performance stability test–Combination 05.

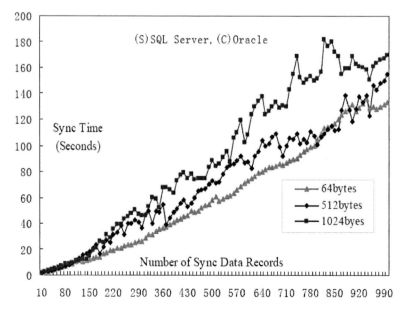

Figure 20. Performance stability test–Combination 06.

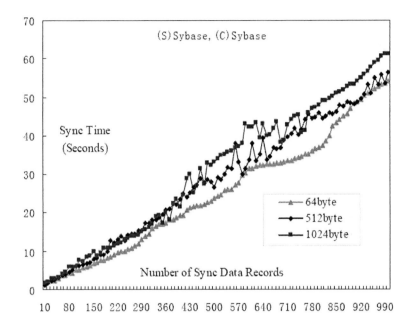

Figure 21. Performance stability test–Combination 07.

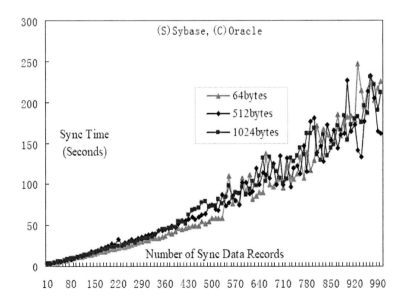

Figure 22. Performance stability test–Combination 08.

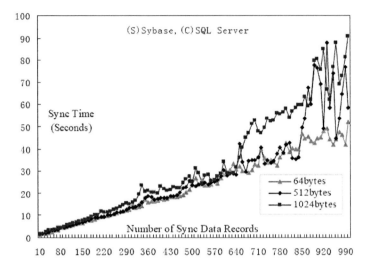

Figure 23. Performance stability test–Combination 09.

15.2. COMPARISON WITH SYNC4J

Sync4j open source system is the first SyncML-compliant data sync middleware, it mainly aims at the data sync requirements of mobile computing and communication fields – in these contexts, the sync data amount is usually small, and the lock-step propagation mechanism could be insignificant. However, in the RDBMS sync applications that involve a large amount of data, their sync processes may fail due to the following sync capacity constraints:

a. Being restricted by the access capacity of the web server, syncs with a huge amount of data would cause traffic jam for accessing server.
b. Being restricted by the disposal capacity of DBMS, concurrent writes with a large of data would probably result in DBMS exceptions.
c. Being restricted by the network transmission capacity, transmissions of large data would encounter a data loss.

In addition, the session mechanism of Sync4j might suffer the following defects:

1. Unable to locate accurately the cause of exceptions, thus it is hard to tackle exceptions appropriately.
2. Unable to resume sync transfer at the abort point when recovering an aborted sync.

As a remedy, Sync4j adopts a very conservative approach for exception handling, that is, it will compulsively assume the slow sync mode for the first resumed sync after any exception, which is for the simplicity of ensuring sync reliability. However, in the case of heavy overhead of DBMS operation and data propagation, the slow sync mode is very inefficient.

For GSMS, we can design and implement a sync capacity adaptation mechanism: according to the sync capacity of the counterpart node of current sync pair, the sync transfer of one data change is divided into several small groups that the transfer is carried out on the basis of one by one group under the lock-step control mode – this is named the *horizontal partition* pattern which is different from the so called *vertical* partition pattern where a record of data is partitioned into several groups of disjoined attributes, and upon the horizontal partition pattern a sync-resuming at abort-point measure is employed further. Since Sync4j can only sync data between homogeneous DBMSs, we have no choice but to make homogenous DBMS sync test comparison between GSMS and Sync4j. The test result comparison indicates that GSMS has a much higher availability and performance than Sync4j, as showed in Figure 24 and 25 for Oracle 9i and MS SQL Sever 2000, respectively.

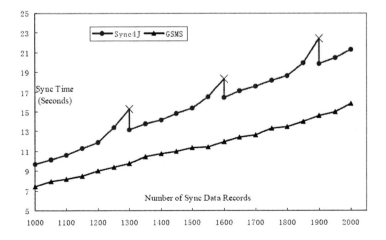

Figure 24. Performance and stability comparison for Sync4j and GSMS (Oracle9i-Oracle9i) [3].

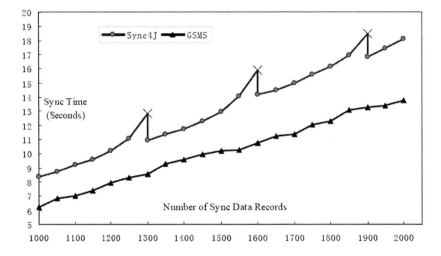

Figure 25. Performance and stability comparison for Sync4j and GSMS (SQL Server-SQL Server).

Chapter 16

CONCLUSION

This chapter has comprehensively discussed DPVT-related issues around the application theme of GSMS product development. The key to eventually-consistent transaction processing lies in that to be realistic, we shall give up the isolation demand for a whole sync transaction, and instead assume a forwards saving-point manner to substitute the atomicity demand, and regard the application acceptance of the eventual consistency as the ultimate target of transactions. This work indicates that practical transaction processing is de facto an issue of software engineering and implementation under the transaction principles, the merits or demerits of a concrete scheme depend on whether the design and realization of software architecture adapts well to the property of domain objects. As to RDBMS products, their normative DML operations, concise formation of data structures, user-defined stored procedures, and built-in trigger mechanism all contribute pro to the connotation of DBMS domain which favors designing a generic DPVT processing system. Utilizing system domain connotation is what we regard the right approach towards developing a practical transaction processing system.

REFERENCES

[1]   Gray, J; Helland, P; O'Neil, P; Shasha, D. The Dangers of Replication And A Solution. *ACM SIGMOD Record*, 1996, 25(2), 173-182.

[2]   Gallersdörfer, R; Nicola, M. Improving performance in replicated database systems through relaxed coherency. *Proc., of 21st VLDB conf.*, 1995, 445-456.

[3]   Haitao Yang, Peng Yang, Pingjing Lu, and Zhenghua Wang. A SyncML Middleware-Based Solution for Pervasive Relational Data Synchronization. *Proceedings of IFIP International Conference on Network and Parallel Computing* (NPC 2008), Shanghai, China, October 2008. J. Cao et al. (Eds.): NPC 2008, LNCS 5245, pp. 308-319, 2008. Doi = 10.1007/978-3-540-88140-7_28.

[4]   Date, CJ. *An Introduction to Database Systems* (7th Ed.), 2000, MA, USA: Addison-Wesley.

[5]   Saito, Y; Shapiro, M. Optimistic replication. *ACM Computing Surveys*, *37(1)*, 2005, 42-81.

[6]   Funambol mobile open source project (earlier known as Sync4j). Cited on 2010-01-18, http://www.funambol.com/opensource/

[7]   Yu, H; Vahdat, A. The costs and limits of availability for replicated services, *ACM Transactions on Computer Systems*, *Vol. 24*, No. 1, Feb. 2006, 70-113.

[8]   Nikaein, N; Bonnet, C. Topology management for improving routing and network performances in mobile ad hoc networks, *Mob. Netw. Appl.*, 2004, 9(6), 583-594.

[9]   Tan, GZ; Han, NN; Liu, Y; Li, JL; Wang, H. Wireless Network Dynamic Topology Routing Protocol Based on Aggregation Tree Model. Int'l Conf. on Netw., *Int'l Conf. on Systems and Int'l Conf. on*

Mobile Comm. and Learning Tech., (ICNICONSMCL'06), 2006, 128-132.

[10] Armendáriz-Iñigo, JE; Decker, H; González de Mendívil, JR; Muñoz-Escoí, FD. Middleware-Based Data Replication: Some History and Future Trends. 2nd Int'l *Workshop on High Availability of Distributed Systems*, 4-8 Sept., 2006, Krakow, Poland. Conf. Proc., 390-394, IEEE-CS Press. *http://doi.ieeecomputersociety.org/10.1109/DEXA.2006.96*

[11] Open Grid Services Architecture — Data Access and Integration (OGSA-DAI). 2007. http://www.ogsa-dai.org.uk

[12] OASIS. *The SyncML Initiative, Technology reports hosted by OASIS,* Last modified: April 29, 2003. http://xml.coverpages.org/syncML.html

[13] Bowling, T; Licul, ED; Hammond, V. Global Data Synchronization — Building a flexible approach. *IBM Business Consulting Services*, 2004. ftp://ftp.software.ibm.com/software/integration/wpc/library/ge-5103990.pdf

[14] Chan, D; Roddick, JF. Summarisation for Mobile Databases, *Journal of Research and Practice in Information Technology*, 2005, Vol. 37, No. 3, 267-284, August.

[15] Bernstein, PA. Middleware: A Model for Distributed System Services. *Communications of ACM*, 1996, 39(2), 86-98, Feb.

[16] Open Mobile Alliance. *SyncML Representation Protocol* (Candidate Version 1.2), June 01, 2004.

[17] Open Mobile Alliance. DS Protocol. *Approved Version*, 2006, 1.2, July 10.

[18] Open Mobile Alliance, SyncML Representation Protocol, Data Synchronization Usage, *Approved Version*, 2006, 1.2, July 10.

[19] Daniels, D; Doo, LB; Downing, A. et al. Oracle's symmetric replication technology and implications for application design. *ACM SIGMOD Record*, 1994, 23(2), 467, June. *http://doi.acm.org/10.1145/ 191839. 191930*

[20] Microsoft. Replication for Microsoft SQL Server Version 7.0. http://msdn.microsoft.com/library/backgrnd/html/msdn_sqlrep.htm,1998

[21] Sybase. Replication Server Administration Guide. Emeryville, CA: Sybase Inc., Dec.1995.

[22] IBM. Replication Guide and Reference (Version 8). Cited on 2010-1-16, ftp://ftp.software.ibm.com/ps/products/db2/info/vr8/pdf/letter/db2e0e80.pdf

[23] Veer, EV. SyncKit White Paper. http://www.synchrologic.com/images/whitepapers/Seybold_white_paper.html, 1998.

[24] Syware. DataSync, a white paper on database replication and synchronization. ttp://www.syware.com/datasync/newdsync/ datasync. htm, 1998.

[25] PeerDirect. PDRE White Papers. http://www.peerdirect.com/products/ Whitepaper/, 1999.

[26] Codd, EF. Further Normalization of the Data Base Relational Model. (Presented at Courant Computer Science Symposia Series 6, "Data Base Systems," New York City, May 24th-25th, 1971.) IBM Research Report RJ909 (August 31st, 1971). Republished in Randall J. Rustin, (Ed.), *Data Base Systems: Courant Computer Science Symposia Series 6.* Prentice-Hall, 1972.

[27] Ullman, JD. *Principles of database systems.* Potomac, MD., USA: Computer Science Press, 1980.

[28] Almeida, PS; Baquero, C; Fonte, V. Version stamps—decentralized version vectors. *Proc. of 22nd Int'l Conf. on Dist. Comp. Sys. (ICDCS)*, Vienna, Austria, 2002, 544-551.

[29] Tel, G. *Introduction to Distributed Algorithms* (2nd Ed.), Cambridge Univ. Press 2000.

[30] Lu Yao, Haitao Yang, Zhenghua Wang, and Peng Yang. Data-sync-capacity adaptation Handling Based on SyncML Protocol. Computer Engineering (in Chinese). 2009, 35 (5), 68-71, 90; ISSN: 1000-3428, CN: 31-1289/TP.

Part II. Relational Representations for Complex Charts

ABSTRACT

In real business practices, charts, due to their intuition and rich expressiveness, have become one of the most common forms accommodating data with indicators. Complex charts usually embody heads for both columns and rows, the structure of such heads could be multi-layered, compound, even very sophisticated – e.g. organized in a forest form, etc., which often cannot be directly stored as relational tables in RDBMS (relational database management system) under its original format. Aiming at how to effectively express such complex charts in relational schemas, this chapter raises an intuitive and facile approach with the merits of being widely-applicable, highly-expressive, and capable of efficient storage.

Chapter 17

INTRODUCTION

In practice, charts (http://en.wikipedia.org/wiki/Chart) are one of the most popular tools of illustrations due to its intuition and rich expressiveness. Charts can appear in a variety of forms, some of them might bear very complex heads – a chart head is referred to the pane of indicators for columns or rows, e.g., the layout of indicators has a forest structure, and may not be stored directly into a relational database system (RDBS) under the original head structure. Regarding almost all commercial database products belong to RDBS, it is essential to find a general approach to map a complex chart into relational schemas provided that the semantics of chart is hold.

In this chapter, the term "chart" covers both digital reports and tabular sheets of text terms – we can name the former "data table", the later "dictionary table", which are different from the relational tables of RDBS. In a broader sense, a data table is a kind of multidimensional data organization. Research literature about transformations between multidimensional data schema and relational data schema mainly comes from the fields of Online Analytical Processing (OLAP), multidimensional databases, and data warehouses, where multidimensional data tables are normally formalized into a data cube or hypercube consisting of dimensions and a measure. Each dimension reflects an index of analysis; the measure stands for the data. The main target of such work is to pull out required data in a prescribed form for computation of aggregation and assort [1,2,3,4]. If multidimensional and relational schemas are interchangeable to each other, the conceptual models of multidimensional databases are orthogonal to their implementations which come down to underlying designs of RDBS products [5]; consequently, related research usually focuses on the topics of mutual representation between multidimensional schema and relational schema, especially on how to create efficiently data cubes for easier analyses [6]. Since data cubes of three and above dimensions are not appropriate for intuitive representations, people usually select two dimensions at a time by assigning the rest dimensions to specific value points in order to focus on how the measure data are influenced by the selected two dimensions – drawing out a chart with two heads (of columns and rows) from records of relational data schemas, which means that data cubes of two dimensions are in most common use. In contrast, there is hardly literature that directly refers to the issue of mapping charts into relational tables, in addition, it often lacks easiness and practicability for using data cube or super-cube models to present charts with complex heads, and further mapping them into relational schemas to store in a RDBS [1,2,4,5,7,8,9,10,11,12]. Therefore, it is necessary to seek convenient, applicable and direct approaches to express charts with complex heads in relational tables.

Chapter 18

TYPICAL RELATIONAL CHARTS

At first, relational tables as the target form of representation should be reviewed briefly on the aspect of semantics reading.

Definition 1. A relational schema *table_name*$<c_1,c_2,...,c_n>$ is referred to as a typical semantic table (**TST**) if, the semantics of its any instance $<a_1,a_2,...,a_n>$ can be explained in one of the following fixed expression,

$$<(c_1 \mid of\ c_1) = a_1, (c_2 \mid of\ c_2) = a_2, ... , (c_n \mid of\ c_n) = a_n> \textbf{ In } table\_name \quad (1)$$

Apparently, there are totally 2^n concrete expressions in the above formula.

Definition 2. A chart is referred to as a typical relational chart (**TRC**) if, it is seen as a direct layout of certain TST in a plane, and its semantics can be expressed by formula (1).

Table 1. List of reconnaissance professionals

Seq	Name	Sex	Age	Tech title/Profession	...
1	Sun Zhang	Male	38	Senior engineer/architect	...
2	Julia Smith	Female	29	Junior engineer/clerk	
...	...			...	

By definition, a **TRC** can be stored in a relational table of RDBS directly under its original logical form while still holding the same semantics, e.g., Table 1 belongs to **TRC**, and the semantics of its first row are:

\<seq = 1, name ="Sun Zhang", sex = "male", ... , > **In** "List of reconnaissance professionals".

Table 2. List of reconnaissance technicians

Seq	Name	Sex	Age	Title	Diploma	Specialty	...
I	Geotechnical Engineering						
1							...
2							
...							
II	Hydrogeology						
19							
...							
III	Engineering Survey						
...							

Table 3. Composition of professionals

Sp \ c		Layout	Architect	Ecology	...	Others	Add up
Total		12	5	3		7	51
Tech-Title	Senior	3	1	1		2	10
	Middle	4	2	1		2	19
	Junior	5	2	1		3	22
Diploma	Post-College	6	2	0		1	13
	College	2	3	2		3	25
	Junior-College	3	0	1		1	9
	Tech-School	1	0	0		2	4
Part-Time		0	1	0		0	3
Retired		0	1	0		1	3

Obviously, charts that do not belong to **TRC** need further study on their expressions in relational data tables – a straight approach is to transfer them into the form of **TRC**. For instance, Table 2 requires a pretreatment of standardization, e.g., adding an attribute name "occupation category" to express the indices of the row head (**RH**). The standardization of Table 3 is similar; where it needs two additional attributes, $a1$ ={"Total", "Tech-Title", "Diploma", "Part-Time", "Retired"} that indicates the 1st layer indices, and $a2$ = {"Senior", "Middle", "Junior", "Post-College", "College", "Junior-College", "Tech-School"} that indicates the 2nd layer index, to present the **RH** indices of depth 2, noticing that some values of $a2$ detail certain values of $a1$, e.g. the {"senior", "middle", "junior"} of $a2$ detail the {"tech-title"} of $a1$. In fact, Table 3 has a **RH** that consists of indices arranged in a forest structure which the classical multidimensional data model and data cube often fails to express.

Chapter 19

RELATIONAL EXPRESSIONS FOR GENERIC CHARTS

19.1. CHARTS OF SINGLE-TIER HEADS

At first we should clearly define those familiar charts as showed in Table 1 and 2.

Definition 3. A regular chart of single-tier heads, in short rcs, has a form as follows,

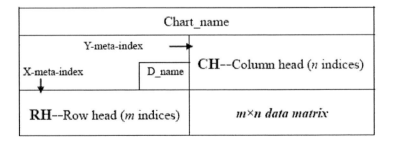

Where, <X-meta-index>, <Y-meta-index>, and <D_name> elements give a generic name respectively for both **RH** and **CH** index lists, and all items from the data matrix. <X-meta-index>, <Y-meta-index>, and <D_name> can be omitted if without any misinterpretation. Hereafter, a **meta-index** is referred to a group of indices regarding their features in common, and in reverse an index is a value of some meta-index. □The simplest chart is a **c**hart of a single head of single-tier (**css**), which can be regarded as a degenerated form of Definition 3:

Definition 4. The regular css form is a degenerated rcs form when <Y-meta-index> and <CH>, or <X-meta-index> and <RH>, as well as <D_name> are removed.

The previous examples have revealed a typical method of transferring rcs into TRC: merging <X-meta-index> into CH, and RH into the data matrix, or merging <Y-meta-index> into RH, and CH into the data matrix.

Definition 5. Row Relation Mapping (*RRM*): given a data matrix M and a relation schema R, each row of M is mapped onto a corresponding tuple of R, denoted as $M \rightarrow^r R$. Column Relation Mapping (*CRM*): each column of M is mapped onto a corresponding tuple of R, i.e., $M \rightarrow^c R$.

From the above definition, we have straightly

Lemma 1. *RRM* (*CRM*) is applicable iif: all elements from the same column (row) are of the same data type.

As to a chart of Definition 3, we have

Definition 6.

1. Row Relation Mapping for a chart with a Single head (*RRM-S*): merging <X-meta-index> into CH as the first element, and RH into the data matrix M as the first column of data, then regard the indices of the new CH as the attributes of a relation schema R, and make $M \rightarrow^r R$.

2. Similarly, Column Relation Mapping for a chart with a Single head (*CRM-S*): merging <Y-meta-index> into RH as the first element, and the indices of CH into the data matrix M as the first row of data, then use the indices of the new RH as the attributes of relation schema R, and make $M \rightarrow^c \boldsymbol{R}$.

Definition 7. Following the convention of OLAP literature [1,2,5,6,8,10], we use "fact table" to refer to the relational schema in which the data matrix of a chart is stored.

Obviously, all parts except <D_name> of rcs can be mapped onto a same relational data table that contains only the original contents of the rcs.

Conclusion 1. If the fact table created by *RRM-S* or *CRM-S* is a TST, and its relational semantics can be labeled with formula (1), then the *RRM-S* or *CRM-S* is semantics-conservable.

Proof. According to Definition 1, the relational semantics of such a fact table has been explained by in the syntax of formula (1), which means that <D_name> can be discarded without causing any misinterpretation. □

Normally element <D_name> is used when the semantics of relational schema takes the form of "of $c_j = a_j$", in this case it can be equivalently used as the suffix or prefix of all attribute names of the schema, or be embodied in a properly modified table name for a one-off handling. For example, in Table 3, suppose that <D_name> = "number" is used as the suffix of all data attribute names, then the first row of the fact table equals to (layout·number=12, architect·number=5, ..., add up·number=51), etc. – these can be reflected by adopting a more proper table name, such as "professional sorted numbers", then <D_name> can be omitted.

However, to hold the semantics entirely and unconditionally, it is advised to use the following relational representation:

Definition 8. Unit Mapping for charts of Single-tier heads (*UM-S*): the target relational schema is <X-meta-index, Y-meta-index, D_name>, for each tuple of which <D_name> is mapped onto by an element of the data matrix, <X-meta-index> and <Y-meta-index> are mapped onto by the RH and CH indices of that element, respectively. □

In *UM-S*, each element of the data matrix corresponds to a unique tuple of the relational schema, e.g., when Table 3 is expressed in relational schema <class, profession, person amount>, then the element located in the first row and first column is mapped onto the tuple <"total", "layout", 12>, its semantics is stated by <class = "Total", profession = "playout", person amount = 12>, similarly, the semantics of element of 6th row and 2nd column is expressed by <class = "diploma·college", profession = "architect", number = 3>. In fact, *UM-S* is a reverse course of *fact table→data cube*, which has the merit of holding the original semantics, however, also the demerit of resulting in the most mapped relational tuples – unfavorably reaching the magnitude of the total number of elements of the data matrix.

Conclusion 2. Given a $m \times n$ data matrix, its onto relational data table has $m \cdot n$ records and $3m \cdot n$ data items for *UM-S*, while only m records and $m(n+1)$ data items for *RRM-S*, and n records and $(m+1)n$ data items for *CRM-S*. By the benchmark of retrieving data items for a row or column of a chart, the efficiency of *UM-S* is a magnitude lower than that of *RRM-S* or *CRM-S* respectively with respect to the number of records searched. □

**Table 4. Professional Configuration
for Enterprise License**

			Structure		Architect		HV&AC	Water Eng.	Electric	Power			Control	...	Budget	Total
License	Register category	Level (Profs number)	Structure(A)	Structure(B)	Architect(A)	Architect(B)	Apparatus (HV&AC)	Apparatus (Water Eng.)	Distribution & supply	Apparatus (Power)				...	Cost	
Industrial certificate		L1	5		3		2	5	3	3	2	3	2	...	3	56
		L2	3			1	1	2	2	2	2	2	1	...	2	29
Profession certification	Waterfeed	L1	4	1	1		1	4	2	3			1	...	2	19
	Waterfeed	L2	2	1		1	1	2	1	2			1	...	2	13
	Waterfeed	L3		1				1	1					...	2	5
	Drain	L1	4	1	1		1	5	3	3			2	...	2	26
	Drain	L2	2	1		1	1	2	2	2			1	...	2	16
	...															

19.2. CHARTS OF MULTI-TIER HEADS

Before going to the cases when charts have a head of irregular multi-tier structure such as Table 4, to which **RRM-S** or **CRM-S** could not be applied directly, we should clearly give at first a definition about the regular multi-tier heads:

Definition 9. A regular **c**hart of **m**ulti-tier heads, in short **rcm**, is as follows,

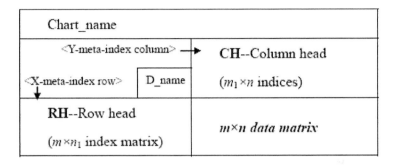

Where, <X-meta-index row> has n_1 meta elements, and each meta element has m indices; <Y-meta-index column> has m_1 meta elements, and each meta element has n indices. □

In nature, charts of regular form are corresponding to multidimensional schema, or data cube (X,Y,Z) in OLAP: X and Y are *dimension*, and Z is called the *measure*, a *dimension* might be composed of several attributes that are referred to as *parameter* [5], the *measure* can also have several attributes. RH corresponds to X *dimension*, CH to Y *dimension*, and <D_name> to the *measure*. To be simple, here we only consider those cases that there is at most one unary data in each element of the data matrix, i.e., all data element are of a single attribute. In fact, data elements of multi-attributes can be identified by a primary key of single attribute, such a primary key should be stored in the data field of fact table, and the multi-attribute data can be stored in another relational schema of <primary key, data tuple>, thereby any multi-attribute measure case can be transferred into a single-attribute case. Intuitively, we have:

Definition 10. Unit Mapping method for charts of Multi-tier heads (*UM-M*): use the relational schema <<X-meta-index row>, <Y-meta-index column>^{T}, D_name> to store elements of the data matrix, where superscript T indicates the matrix transpose.

The *RRM-S* in the previous section shows the kernel idea of row relation mapping: merging RH matrix into the data matrix, and then apply **RRM** to the new data matrix. To this stage, the matter is about how to express **CH** of multi-tier with relational attributes of single-tier. Of course, if any (m_1-1) tiers indices of CH can be merged into the data matrix, then the case has come down to that of the single-tier head already. As Lemma 1 stated, however, usually it does not work since the data type of an index name is often different from that of the corresponding element column of the original data matrix.

Definition 11. Given a chart of multi-tier heads, as defined by Definition 9, for which the Row Relation Mapping, in short *RRM-M*, is defined as: 1) merging the index matrix of RH into the data matrix as the first n_1 columns, and n_1 meta elements of <X-meta-index> into CH as the indices for the first n_1 columns of the resulted data matrix M, respectively; 2) assign a *nickname* (normally in a character string) to each index column of the new CH, and use these *nicknames* as attribute names to construct a relational schema R; 3) apply $M \rightarrow^r R$. Accordingly, the Column Relation Mapping, in short *CRM-M*, can be similarly defined – it is omitted for simplification.

UM-M is intuitive and easy to use, but has a higher overhead compared with *RRM-M* or *CRM-M* (refer to Conclusion 2). Besides, charts of irregular forms are also quite common, e.g., in nature both heads of Table 4 have a structure of forest, which cannot be put into the regular mold unless undergoing a rearrangement – some units of CH need splitting, for instance, the "Structure" unit should be split vertically into three identical horizontal units, the "Total" should be split horizontally into the upper unit and the lower unit, etc. Therefore, it is required to consider a more general form of charts:

Definition 12. A chart of index Forest heads, in short, ciF, is as:

Chart_name		
Data	**CH (Column head) index forest**	
	n Leaves … …	
RH (Row head) index forest	*m* Leaves…	data matrix $\left\{ a_{ij} \right\}_{m \times n}$

Where, each data element corresponds to a unique tuple of **RH** and **CH**: given that R_i is the *i*-th leaf of **RH** index forest, and C_j is the *j*-th leaf of **CH** index forest, then the matrix element a_{ij} is identified or located by the tuple $<R_i, C_j>$ one-one. □

Apparently, we cannot apply a unit mapping directly to the charts that have heads of index forest unless their heads have been transferred into the regular form of index matrixes. To be simple, hereafter we only approach to dispose of index forest for CH since the approach for RH is similar.

Equivalent index Matrix for a forest head (*EiMf*): introduce a list of meta-index such as <1st tier index>, <2nd tier index>, ... , <n^{th} tier index>, here *n* stands for the height (the biggest level number) of the highest tree, say T is an index tree of height *h* in the index forest of CH, f_k is a leaf on the *k* level of T with ($k \leq h$), the path from the root down to f_k is $f_1 f_2 ... f_{k-1} f_k$, then map the path onto a column $(c_1, c_2, ..., c_n)^T$ of the result matrix such that $(\forall i \leq k)c_i = f_i$, $(\forall i > k)c_i$=null. □

The reverse transformation is also possible – a hierarchy head where each tier may hold a different number of units, a form more general than matrix, can be transformed into the form of index forest, see the follow,

Equivalent index Forest for a hierarchy head (*EiFh*): number all tiers downwards from the top by a number sequence of {1,2,...,n}, traverse all paths from the *n*-th tier up to the first tier, present each path in a form of $L(1) \cdot L(2) ... \cdot L(n-1) \cdot L(n)$ with the L(*i*) item stands for the name of the passed index on the *i*-th tier, and then regard items of the path expression from the left to the right orderly as the nodes of a branch that span from the root down to the leaf of a tree – each index of the path corresponds to a unique node of the tree. □

Regarding the above two transformations for equivalent expression, *EiMf* and *EiFh*, from the standpoint of holding semantics we have

Conclusion 3. The process of applying *EiMf* to the heads of a ciF does not hold the original semantics of the ciF in general, whereas that of applying *EiFh* to a chart of hierarchy heads does.

Proof. Formally, an index tree assign a parent-child relation to the adjacent supper and lower tiers, e.g., as shown in Table 4, the index of "Register category" should belong to an index of the supper-tier "Specialty", but, relation tuples for a list of meta-index mean nothing similar. Contrarily, the concatenation of adjacent indices lined in several adjacent tiers certainly holds the original hierarchy relationship, and via indices' connections to their common ancestors the relationships between indices along the horizontal direction are maintained. □

Since a multidimensional table is equivalent to an **rcm**, and **rcm** is only a subtype of **ciF**, therefore, as for semantics conservation the relation-schema representations for **ciF** may exceed the expression capacity of classical multidimensional data models including OLAP data cubes.

19.3. CHARTS OF FOREST HEADS

Relational schema representations had better take both semantics conservation and storage efficiency into account. To increase storage efficiency, referring to conclusion 2, we hope to find a row or column relation mapping method for ciF. An intuitive idea may come like this: at first manage to eliminate one head, and then compress the rest head into one tier – the parent index is used as the prefix of child indices, each prefix is separated by symbol "·", after all prefixes are attached to the primitive name of the leaf index, we get a full-prefix name for that leaf index. Such a prefixing process is named head-compression, in short H-C. For example, via H-C the multi-tier RH of Table 3 is compressed into a single tier one as a list of full-prefix names: {"Tech-Title·Senior", "Tech-Title·Middle", "Tech-Title·Junior", "Diploma·Post-College", "Diploma·College", "Diploma·Junior-College", "Diploma·School"}; the RH of Table 4 is compressed into a single tier as an index list of {"Industrial certificate·L1", "Industrial certificate·L2", "Profession certification·Waterfeed·L1", "Profession certification·Waterfeed·L2", "Profession certification·Waterfeed·L3", "Profession certification·Drain·L1", ...}. Reviewing the conclusion 3, similarly we have,

Conclusion 4. The process that compresses an index forest head of a char into a single-tier consisting of the full-prefix names of the index tree's leaves is of semantics conservation. □

Definition 13. Row Relation Mapping for ciF, in short *RRM-F*: 1) translate the index forest of RH into an index matrix, and apply *RRM* to such an index matrix, resulting <relational schema of RH>; 2) get a full-prefix name for each leaf of the index forest of CH, and assign a nickname to each full-prefix name, and then use these nicknames as attribute names to construct <relational schema of the data matrix> such that each attribute labels a specific data column (of the data matrix) indicated by the corresponding leaf index; 3) use <<relational schema of RH>, <relational schema of the data matrix>> as the relational schema of the fact table for the original chart; 4) define a table named *attribute-table* in the relational schema <nickname, leaf full-prefix name> to detail the semantics of each attribute of the fact table under a nickname.

Adopting directly full-prefix names as attribute names should be avoided since there is usually a length constraint set by DBMS on attribute name.

Definition 14. Row Relation Mapping via H-C for ciF, in short *RRMc-F*: 1) compress the index forest of RH into a single-tier head consisting of full-prefix names of RH's all leaves, and use an element <row meta-index> to indicate such a single-tier head; 2) give each leaf of the index forest of CH a full-prefix name, assign each full-prefix name a unique nickname, and use these nicknames as the names of attributes that construct <relational schema of data matrix>, in which each attribute labels a data column (of the data matrix) indicated by the corresponding leaf index; 3) use the attribute tuple <<row meta-index>, <relational schema of data matrix>> as the relational schema of the fact table of the original chart; 4) define a table named *attribute-table* in the relational schema <nickname, leaf full-prefix name> to detail the semantics of each attribute of the fact table under a nickname. □

The Column Relation Mapping via H-C can be defined similarly, however, which is omitted here for avoiding verbosity. Besides, basing on H-C, we raise

Definition 15. Unit Mapping via H-C for ciF, in short *UMhc-F*: 1) compress the index forest of RH into a single-tier head RH-1 that consists of full-prefix names of RH's all leaves, assign a nickname for each of these full-prefix names, and use these nicknames as the values of <row meta-index> to indicate RH-1; 2) compress the index forest of CH into a single-tier head CH-1 that consists of full-prefix names of CH's all leaves, assign a nickname for each of these full-prefix names, and use these nicknames as the values of <column meta-index> to indicate CH-1; 3) adopt the attribute tuple <<row meta-index>, <column meta-index>,<D_name>> as the fact table's relational schema for the original chart; 4) define an table name *attribute-table* in the relational schema <nickname, leaf full-prefix name> to detail the semantics of each attribute of the fact table under a nickname.

Although the above approaches of relation schema mapping via H-C have the advantage of semantics conservation, they are not suitable for grouping and aggregation calculations of SQL queries since multiple dimensions are compressed into one-dimension. As to the reverse process of mapping a relational schema back to the chart, we can regain the index forest by comparing prefix strings of leaf full-prefix names.

Regarding various lengths of leaf full-prefix names, some extreme cases might result a low efficiency of storage for schema <nickname, leaf full-prefix name>, we suggest another schema instead: <nickname, H-code, index name>, where, <index name> stores only the primitive name but any prefix for an index with respect to a single tier, <nickname> = *null* indicates that the corresponding index is not an attribute of the fact table, but a non-leaf index, and <H-code> is defined as follows,

Definition 16. H-code: given an index forest $F\{T_1,T_2,...,T_n\}$, a node q on the j-th tier of tree T_i with k tiers, we use a series of segment codes $S_1 \cdot S_2 \cdot ... \cdot S_j$ to express q, in which for $k \geq j > 1$ the $(j-1)$-th segment code S_{j-1} is the code of q's parent node on the $(j-1)$-th tier, and S_1 is the code of the root node of T_i. All root nodes of trees from F are coded uniformly.

By introducing H-code, the restoration process from the fact table and *attribute-table* is that: look up a leaf index's name and its H-code by the nickname, then from the right jump to left, segment by segment using the current prefix of the leaf index's H-code to locate the name of each ancestor index of the leaf index upwards in sequence.

Conclusion 5. Given that the average number of tiers of table heads is K, the average length of index names is L, the data matrix has m rows and n column, then we have: 1) regarding the fact table only, UM (*UM-M* or *UM-S*) needs more storage than *RRM* by $K \cdot L \cdot m \cdot n$ bytes; 2) if using a H-code method to implement the *attribute-table* under the condition that, lengths of nicknames do not exceed the average segment length of H-codes, C, and the non-null ratio of the data matrix's elements is ρ, and then, even if UM does not map any element of null value, it still needs more storage than *RRM* at least by $\rho \cdot K \cdot L \cdot m \cdot n - K \cdot n \cdot (L+(K+1)C)$ bytes.

Proof. 1) As to each element of the data matrix, UM will store names of indices from every tier of the index column affiliated to the resulted fact table, but *RRM* wouldn't, therefore, UM will on average use additional $K \cdot L$ bytes than RM to store each data element. 2) Regarding that RM has an additional attribute table which needs a storage no greater than $K \cdot n \cdot (L+(K+1)C)$ bytes. □

This shows that, although the storage efficiency of UM will be improved for a lower ρ, i.e., a higher degree of sparsity of the data matrix, e.g., as in Table 4, but the inequality $(K+1)C \leq L \wedge \rho \cdot m \geq 2$ often holds, which implies UM's overhead is higher than RM's.

We can further extend the above approaches to charts with net-structure heads. First, we give related definitions as the follows,

Definition 17. An Undirected Connected Simple Graph, in short *UCSG*, $G=<V,E>$ is referred to as *thread-via* V_1 if: 1) $V_1 \subseteq V$, the sub-graph of G induced by V_1 is a forest, and any vertex of V_1 has no parents in $V'_1=V-V_1$; 2) $\forall y \in V'_1$, if $(\exists x \in V_1) \Rightarrow x-y \in E$, where $x-y$ stands an edge connecting vertex x and y, then y has no parents in V'_1.

Definition 18. Given a *UCSG* of G=<V,E> *thread-via* V_1, $\forall y \in V-V_1$, if $\exists x \in V_1 \Rightarrow x\text{-}y \in E$, then x is called a parent of y, denoted as $(x \rightarrow y)$, V_1 is called an elder of y, denoted as $(V_1 \rightarrow y)$, the set of parents of y is denoted as $p_a(y)=\{x|x \in V_1, x\text{-}y \in E\}$.

Definition 19. A *UCSG* of G=<V,E> is referred to as *thread-via* $V_1 \rightarrow V_2$ if:

1. *Thread-via* V_1;
2. Let $V'_1=V-V_1$, $\forall y \in V'_1 \wedge (V_1 \rightarrow y) \Rightarrow$ duplicate y and its adjacent edges for $|p_a(y)|\text{-}1$ times, thus get $|p_a(y)|$ copies of node y and its connections, and then trim all edges that connect these copies of y to V_1 such that each copy of y has only one adjacent edge connecting to its elder V_1, and different copies connect to a different parent of y in V_1, which is called the trimming step.
3. Denote the above processed G=<V,E> as $hr(G)=<V^{(1)},E^{(1)}>$, let $V^+_1= \{x|x \in (V^{(1)}\text{-}V_1) \wedge (\exists y \in V_1)(x\text{-}y \in E^{(1)})\}$, $V_2=V_1 \cup V^+_1$, then $hr(G)$ is *thread-via* V_2.

The above process is denoted as $G(V_1) \rightarrow hr(G)(V_2)$, and V_1 is referred to as the upper-tier of V^+_1, while V^+_1 is referred to as the under-tier of V_1. □

Definition 19. A *UCSG* of G=<V,E> is regarded *hierarchicable* if: there are $G(V_1) \rightarrow hr(G)(V_2)$, $hr(G)(V_2) \rightarrow hr^2(G)(V_3)$, …, $hr^i(G)(V_{i+1}) \rightarrow hr^{i+1}(G)(V_{i+2})$, and $V_{i+1}=V_{i+2}$, where, $hr^i(G) = \underbrace{hr(hr(...(hr(G))...))}_{hr \text{ appears } i \text{ times}}$. V_{i+1} is called the final thread. □

Conclusion 6. Given a *UCSG* G of indices from a chart, which is created with each index as a vertex and each connection between indices as an edge, if any connected sub-graph of G is *hierarchical*, then we have: 1) G can be transformed into a forest while conserving the original connections between indices; 2) all the paths in G are retained during the process of transformation – a hierarchizing process.

Proof. Assuming a process defined by Definition 19 as the transformation method, then we have: 1) by definition, the final thread resulted by the process must be a forest, and there is no any vertex outside the final thread – otherwise, the final sub-graph is an unconnected graph, a contradiction arise; 2) because G is a simple graph, the set of paths passing a duplicated vertex remains unchanged through the trimming step regarding that replicas from a same source vertex could be considered semantics-identical. □

So far, we can see that all relational schema mappings in this section can be applied to a chart with net-structure heads provided that the table's heads can be transformed into an index forest form, Figure 1 shows a simple example of hierarchical net-structure index graph.

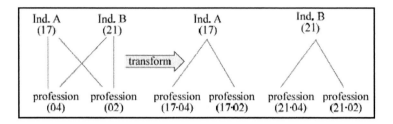

Figure 1. Hierarchizing a graph of net-structure.

Chapter 20

COMPARISON WITH RELATED WORK

Disposals of charts of multi-tier heads can be traced back to the research of multi-dimensional data models (MDDM); however, classical MDDMs lack the capacity of expressing charts of complex heads, such as heads of index forest, net-structure, and non-hierarchy – not exists a partial-order relation between indices from vertically-adjacent tiers (e.g., the higher tier is an abstraction of the lower tier), etc. To the best of our knowledge, traditional MDDMs [2,5] that regard the *measure* as a point in a multidimensional space have no concepts and semantics about layering dimension, while the extended MDDMs [10,9,8,4,12] that support the structures of dimension-layering are in short of adaptation capacity, e.g., those raised by literature [4], which are based on partial-order, are not suitable for non-hierarchical heads, those put by [12] cannot express index heads of forest structures, not to mention the net-structure's. First of all, we should point out that the dimension structures that MDDMs concern are normally limited to the scope of connections between attributes of the same dimension, and in case exists connections between attributes from different dimensions, it would suggest that these attributes should be combined into the same dimension [11]; secondly, MDDMs' attribute relation analysis is not on the attribute level but on the element level of value sets of attributes [11,12] – which value elements are correlated, and how they are correlated, e.g., in partial-order, functional dependency, etc.; if the values of an attribute can be classified into more detailed categories, then it is recommended to divide such an attribute into several attributes further. The processes that base on sets of attributes' values often make the *fact table* in RDBMS sparse – detailed attributes may produce data records such that some attributes can only have a null value while other have a meaningful value, this sophisticates the disposal of relational schema representation, and is also against semantics conservation. Nevertheless, the schemes raised in this chapter can easily handle charts of complex heads, including index forest or net-structure heads, and are intuitive and pellucid, especially regarding that understandability is a key metric for evaluating MDDM [13].

Besides, MDDM's focus on data sets of same dimensions, and their methods are usually not apt for data matrix with index forests. OLAP process mainly concerns with aggregating and grouping calculations and their further details or generalizations, such as, SQL queries of *count, average, sum, group by, ...,* and *roll-up* or *drill-down,* etc [2,3,4,7]. Whereas the charts studied in this chapter are already the analysis results or regulated illustrations of business data or contents, they are mainly used for queries: seeking or locating entries in the data matrix under certain indices of chart heads, needless to refer to those aggregating or grouping computations.

Chapter 21

CONCLUSION

Due to the powerful expressiveness and intuitiveness of charts, people are often willing to use them to present data reports, codes or rules, index systems, etc.; they are widely applied in a variety of business affairs. Formal definitions introduced in this chapter for usual charts, especially for those with complex head structures, are concise, intuitive, and easily understood, and the raised relational schema representations for typical charts are widely applicable and operational, and apt to implementation; they all have a significant value of direct applications in relational database modeling around business charts.

REFERENCES

[1] P.M. Lewis, A. Bernstein, and M. Kifer. Databases and Transaction Processing: An Application-Oriented Approach. Beijing: Pearson Education North Asia Limited and Higher Education Press, Oct. 2002, pp. 643-665.

[2] J. Gray, S. Chaudhuri, A Bosworth, A. Layman, D. Reichart, M. Venkatrao, F. Pellow, and H. Pirahesh. Data Cube: A Relational Aggregation Operator Generalizing Group-By, Cross-Tab, and Sub-Totals. *Data Mining and Knowledge Discovery*, Vol.1, 1997, pp. 29–53.

[3] A. Savinov. Grouping and Aggregation in the Concept-Oriented Data Model. Proc. 2006 ACM Symposium on Applied Computing (Dijon, France, April 23-27, 2006). New York, NY: ACM Press, 2006, pp.482-486. DOI= http://doi.acm.org/10.1145/ 1141277.1141390

[4] T.B. Pedersen, C.S. Jensen, and C.E. Dyreson. A Foundation for Capturing and Querying Complex Multidimensional Data. Information Systems, 2001, 26 (5): 383-423.

[5] M. Gyssens and L.V.S. Lakshmanan. A Foundation for Multidimensional Databases. Proc. 23rd Conf. on Very Large Databases, 1997, pp. 106-115.

[6] http://en.wikipedia.org/wiki/OLAP_cube

[7] A. Abelló, J. Samos, and F. Saltor. A Framework for the Classification and Description of Multidimensional Data Models. Proc. 12th Int'l. Conf. on Database and Expert Systems Applications (DEXA 2001), H.C. Mayr, et al, Eds. LNCS 2113, Berlin Heidelberg: Springer-Verlag, 2001, pp. 668–677.

[8] T.B. Pederson and C.S. Jensen. Multidimensional Data Modeling for Complex Data. Proc. 15th International Conference on Data

Engineering, M. Kitsuregawa, L. Masiaszek, M. Papazoglou, et al, Eds. Los Alamitos, CA: IEEE Society Press, 1999, pp. 336-345.

[9]   W. Lehner. Modeling Larger Scale OLAP Scenarios. Proc. 6th International Conference on Extending Database Technology, G. Jorh and I. Ramos, Eds. New York: Springer-Verlag, 1998, pp: 153-167.

[10] R. Agrawal, A. Gupta, and S. Sarawagi. Modeling Multidimensional Databases. Proc. 13th International Conference on Data Engineering, M. Jackson and C. Pu, Eds. Los Alamitos, CA: IEEE Society Press, 1997, pp. 105-116.

[11] N. Spyratos. A Functional Model for Data Analysis. Proc. 7th Int'l. Conf. on Flexible Query Answering Systems (FQAS 2006), H.L. Larsen, et al, Eds. LNAI 4027, Berlin Heidelberg: Springer-Verlag, 2006, pp. 51-64.

[12] E. Malinowski and E. Zimányi. Hierarchies in a Multidimensional Model: from Conceptual Modeling to Logical Representation. Data & Knowledge Engineering, 2006, 59(2): 348-377.

[13] M. Serrano, J. Trujillo, C. Calero, and M. Piattini. Metrics for Data Warehouse Conceptual Models Understandability. Information and Software Technology, 2007, 49(8): 851-870.

INDEX